Original title:
Icebound Reflections

Author: Colin Harrington
ISBN HARDBACK: 978-9916-94-474-5
ISBN PAPERBACK: 978-9916-94-475-2

The Beauty of Solitude

In a room with socks unmatched,
I ponder life and snacks attached.
The cat meows a funny tune,
As I gaze out at the moon.

A cup of tea and slippers wide,
Confessions made to walls I bide.
Talking to my own reflection,
He laughs back, what a connection!

A dance party with my broom,
Dust bunnies swirl in my living room.
I trip and laugh, it’s such a sight,
Solo fun feels just so right.

The vacuum hums, my loyal friend,
In this madness, I can depend.
A sandwich dropped, oh what a fuss,
I’ll share my meal, just me and dust!

Whispers of the Winter Sky

The clouds are fluffy marshmallows,
Dancing in the chilly blue,
With each breath, we make big puffs,
Our laughter falls like snowflakes too.

Squirrels wear their winter coats,
Chasing snowflakes, what a sight!
They slip and slide on icy paths,
But they think it’s pure delight.

A Frosted Portrait

The trees are dressed in glittering white,
Like nature’s own party, what a show!
Snowmen wink with carrot noses,
As children giggle, cheeks aglow.

Old man Winter paints with glee,
His brush spills sparkles everywhere,
But he can't stop a snowball fight,
Watch out! Those snowballs fly through air!

The Quiet of the Frozen World

In the hush, a snowman sighs,
Telling tales of winter lore,
He says, ‘Chill out, take a break,
I’ve got plenty of snow to score.’

Birds in sweaters hop about,
Searching for a snack or two,
They clink like ice in festive glass,
While we sit and sip our brew.

Ephemeral Brightness

Sunlight dances on each flake,
Turning frosty glass to gold,
Even penguins laugh and slide,
As the warmth begins to unfold.

But don’t get too comfy dear friend,
Winter waits, it’s just a tease,
With a wink, she’ll come back around,
And freeze your toes with icy breeze!

The Hush of the Icy Evenfall

Snowflakes dance like little spies,
Layering secrets 'neath the skies.
Frosty breath in the chilly air,
Whispers of laughter everywhere.

Squirrels in sweaters, looking chic,
Chattering nonsense, oh so unique.
Penguins parade with wobbly grace,
In a frozen world, it's a funny place.

Shimmer of the Frozen Stars

Stars are twinkling like frosty gems,
While snowmen giggle at winter's hems.
A bowl of soup and a joyful grin,
In the cold, we let the warmth begin.

Chill in the air, but spirits are bright,
Warm mittens offered in funny fights.
Riding sleds like rockets on the ice,
Laughter echoes, isn’t that nice?

Reflections on a Frigid Surface

Puddles glisten, a slippery prank,
Watch out for folks who may fall, crank!
Mirrors of laughter, frozen surprise,
Wobbly reflections make for good times.

A dog in boots leaps in delight,
Chasing his tail in the pale moonlight.
What a sight! With giggles so loud,
As snow starts to make us all proud.

An Elegy in Ice

A snowman's hat took a wild flight,
Chasing a rabbit that's out all night.
In chilly defeat, the snowman sighs,
What's winter fun without a few cries?

Frosty fables float through the air,
With playful whispers hidden everywhere.
Clumsy love in an Arctic dance,
Oh freeze the moment—give life a chance!

Glittering Veils of Slumber

In the land of chilly dreams,
Where penguins wear bright costumes,
Snowflakes dance with silly glee,
A snowman sings in funny tunes.

Under blankets thick as cakes,
Fluffy pillows join the play,
Hot cocoa spills, it's quite a mess,
As winter laughs and melts away.

A Portrait of Frost

The windows wear their frosty art,
A smile drawn from a chilly heart,
Carrots stuck with glowing pride,
Snow-white cheeks that cannot hide.

A painter slips on icy trails,
His palette filled with snowy tales,
With each brush stroke a frosty tickle,
His canvas giggles, oh so fickle.

Silenced by the Chill

The wind whispers jokes through the pines,
A squirrel chuckles at wild designs,
Trembling trees in a frozen sway,
Laughing leaves have gone astray.

Snowflakes tumble in gleeful spins,
Each one daring the cold to win,
"Catch me if you can!" they play,
A flurry of chuckles on display.

Delicate Frosted Reflections

In the mirror, what do we see?
A cheeky rabbit sipping tea,
His whiskers frosted, eyes aglow,
Laughing softly at the show.

A reflective pond begins to crack,
As frogs proclaim, “Let’s race back!”
With leaps and hops they laugh and cheer,
Creating bubbles, spreading cheer.

Whispers of the Frozen Mind

Snowflakes dance on frozen ponds,
Making friends with chatty swans.
A squirrel slips on ice with flair,
Finding his balance in mid-air.

The muffled laughs of winter's chill,
As penguins strut, they surely thrill.
Frosty jokes float on the breeze,
Like snowmen sneezing in the trees.

Portraits in a Shivering Landscape

A snowman poses, scarf awry,
"Too hot" he laughs, but he can't lie.
Chattering teeth in chilly frost,
With every breath, a mist, embossed.

In winter's grip, the trees all sway,
While shivering birds sing out, "Hooray!"
Each flake a tiny work of art,
Some land on noses—oh, the smart!

Still Waters of the Winter’s Veil

Mirror lakes that gleam and glint,
Catch a crooked grin, not a hint.
A duck attempts a graceful dive,
Then flops and splashes—it’s alive!

Reflections giggle all around,
As shadows dance upon the ground.
In winter’s realm, where laughter flows,
The frozen jokes are all that grow.

Chilling Dreams of Reflected Stars

Under starry skies so bright,
Snowmen dream of snowball fights.
An owl hoots at midnight's glee,
“Who’s out there? Is it just me?”

The moon winks down, so round and wide,
While snowflakes whirl and spin with pride.
The world between is quirky, cold,
Where laughter warms this tale retold.

A Tapestry of Frost and Whispered Thoughts

In the chill of the morning frost,
Penguins slide, dodging what they've lost.
Snowmen grin with carrot nose,
While snowflakes dance in funny clothes.

Hot cocoa spills on thermal wear,
As laughter rings through the frozen air.
Sledding down hills, the thrill is grand,
With rosy cheeks and outstretched hands.

Frosty windows, a canvas bright,
Drawing smiles in the pale moonlight.
In a world where giggles freeze,
Joy's found amidst the winter breeze.

The Beauty in Winter’s Embrace

Snowflakes twirl like dervishes bold,
As mittens fumble, tales unfold.
A snowball fight, a cheeky aim,
Laughter echoes—a winter game.

Chilling winds with playful glee,
Whisper secrets, 'Come play with me!'
Icicles hang like nature's chimes,
Creating symphonies in frosty climes.

Hot soup spills with every fall,
As sleds collide—a winter brawl.
Underneath the stars so bright,
We dance with shadows under moonlight.

Frozen Echoes

In the woods a squirrel darts,
Belly flops and winter arts.
Snowmen wobble, hats askew,
Drawing giggles from the crew.

Snowballs whizz, a cold surprise,
As laughter sparkles, joy complies.
Frothy mugs held high in cheer,
Winter's fun is truly here!

Pinecones tumble, laughter swells,
Frostbit limbs tell silly tales.
In the glimmer of the snow,
Chilled delights make spirits glow.

Shattered Glimmers

With every step, the ice does crack,
Like giggles held, a little whack.
Snowflakes wink and tease the crowd,
In every flurry, laughter loud.

Skating shoes that dare to slip,
Causing many a funny trip.
Frosty beards on each face,
Adding to winter's quirky grace.

Fluffy boots stomp in delight,
As winter games turn day to night.
Reflections caught in cold and clear,
Winter's joy spreads far and near.

The Stillness Between Moments

In the chill of frosty air,
I slip on ice without a care,
My dog just laughs, what a sight,
As I cling to the ground, feeling light.

Snowflakes giggle, swirl and dance,
While I try to maintain my stance,
The ground is slick, my socks are wet,
Oh, winter, my silliest pet!

Timeless Frost

Chattering teeth in the morning light,
I swear that snow has taken flight,
Mirrors frost my balmy smile,
As I slide for quite a while!

Beneath the chill, I'm bundled tight,
A snowman grins with pure delight,
He asks for coffee; I chuckle back,
In winter's world, sanity I lack!

The Lullaby of Winter's Breath

Snowflakes serenade the ground,
With frosty whispers, soft and sound,
Hot cocoa waits, to warm my toes,
But outside? A snowball fight in rows!

A snow angel plops, without a care,
As I wipe off frost from my hair,
The world’s a chuckle, wrapped in white,
Where winter’s breath ignites delight!

Ever After in Cold

In a land where boots march left and right,
And mittens wave in frosty fight,
I twirl like a penguin, arms spread wide,
Slipping, tripping, but filled with pride.

As icicles dangle like a frozen cheer,
I know summer will always reappear,
But for now, I'll dance in frozen fun,
And laugh as winter's mischief has begun!

Frosted Dreams

In a world of frozen treats,
I slip on yonder winter's sweets.
A penguin dances with a grin,
He asked me if I'd let him in.

Snowflakes fall like silly hats,
Each one a prank from playful cats.
I built a snowman with a twist,
He waved goodbye, I think he missed.

Winter's cold, but I don't care,
I'm wrapped in layers everywhere.
My hot cocoa begins to freeze,
While squirrels laugh and tease the bees.

Dreams of warmth and sunshine bright,
Oh how I long for summer's light.
But here I’m stuck in frosty fun,
With winter’s winks and icy puns.

Beneath a Hollow Sky

Beneath a sky of frosty blue,
I spotted something strange, it's true.
A snowman’s hat took flight above,
Could it be Cupid's lost white glove?

A polar bear in shades just struts,
While penguins play their silly guts.
They roller skate on frozen ponds,
And giggle at the frozen swans.

I found a snowball that could speak,
It told me jokes from cheek to cheek.
I laughed so hard, I lost my mitt,
But winter’s chill just wouldn’t quit.

So here I sit with frosty friends,
With every laugh, the cold descends.
We'll play until the sun's awake,
And hope that we don't catch a break!

Chilling Whispers

Chilling whispers in the breeze,
Snowflakes fly like sneaky keys.
A frosty breeze sings lullabies,
While icicles are drumming sly.

I tried to catch a snowball's toss,
But landed smack—what a great loss!
The snowman giggled in delight,
While squirrels laughed, oh what a sight!

Frosty trees with twinkling lights,
Dance around like winter sprites.
I tripped over a sleeping fox,
And landed in a box of socks!

Riding sleds with friendly glee,
We crash and roll, oh joy for me!
With chilly chuckles filling air,
We'll frolic on without a care.

Glacial Reverie

Glacial dreams of frosty fun,
Chasing shadows, everyone!
I twirled and slipped, a silly dance,
Oh look, a snowball's got the chance!

Puddles frozen, slips abound,
With laughter echoing all around.
A snow dog barks at frozen stars,
While penguins race their tiny cars.

Each snowflake whispers silly rhymes,
With every fall, I lose my climes.
Frosty friends begin to cheer,
They say "It's winter—have no fear!"

As icy breezes tease my nose,
I dream of warming up in prose.
Yet here I stay in a frosty trance,
In winter’s grip, my heart’s in dance.

Winter's Quiet Contemplation

Snowflakes dance and swirl around,
While penguins strut with grace profound.
Frosty breath in chilly air,
Why does everyone stop and stare?

Hot cocoa spills, oh what a mess!
Laughter echoes, we must confess.
The snowman’s hat, it’s just too tall,
He tips now, we all start to fall!

Winter nights with cozy socks,
Chasing shadows, dodging flocks.
Icicles hanging from the eaves,
Like nature’s shiv, making us grieve!

But oh the joy in frosty fun,
With each snowball, we've surely won.
A winter's day, let’s play awhile,
And make the world a frosty smile!

The Frozen Tale

Once a snowman wore a frown,
When the kids began to clown.
With a carrot nose, he blurted 'Hey!'
'This is not the game to play!'

Snow would fly and voices chirp,
As sledding caused a snowy slurp.
Froze the pond? What a surprise!
Flat on my back, under blue skies!

Penguins waddled up to chat,
'This weather's fine, imagine that!'
They laughed at all our silly slips,
And danced in their freezing, floating quips!

We built a fort, oh what a feat,
With victory snacks, we had a treat.
In frozen lands, our laughter peeled,
In winter's arms, our joy was sealed!

Traces in the Frost

Little footprints in white powdered snow,
Who knew a snowball could fly so low?
Sledding down hills, we chase the sun,
Rolling in snow, oh what fun!

Frosted laughter fills the air,
Snowflakes ride on friends' wild hair.
Hot chocolate spills down my sleeve,
I guess I'm just meant to weave!

Chasing shivers, we zigzag fast,
We're wondering how long this fun can last.
Giggling snow angels, flapping about,
One fell flat, and there's no doubt!

Now back inside, the fireplace glows,
With every drink, our laughter grows.
Winter tales told with flair,
Ignite our hearts in chilly air!

January Reveries

January brings a snowy tease,
With penguins gliding with utmost ease.
Everyone slips, it's quite a scene,
In snowdrifts, we break out the cuisine!

Frosty noses and silly hats,
We're fashionistas, look at that!
Snowflakes fall, each one unique,
Yet all of us, we can’t quite speak!

The snowball fights begin anew,
With every toss, I scream ‘Look out! You!’
We tumble and roll, what a delight,
In icy realms, we take flight!

Now the sun peeks through the freeze,
We swap our tales with merry ease.
Winter’s whimsy lingers near,
Through snow-covered laughter, we cheer!

The Quietude of Frosted Dawn

The sun peeks out, all shy and meek,
Snowflakes dance, like little freaks.
A squirrel slips on a frosty slide,
While penguins brag about their glide.

Morning whispers, with a chilly laugh,
Snowmen plotting their silly craft.
One has a carrot, but it’s askew,
He dreams of being a chef at a stew.

Frosty air and giggles blend,
As warm breath puffs and starts to bend.
A snowball flies with a whoosh and zap,
And lands right on a snoozing chap.

With chattering teeth and rosy nose,
Winter's fun is anything but prose.
Amidst the chill, laughter takes flight,
In this wintry wonder, everything's bright.

Frigid Faces of a Crystal World

In a world where icicles grow on trees,
Frogs wear scarves for a winter breeze.
Snowmen argue about their hats,
While ducks are dressed like adorable spats.

Chattering critters in furry coats,
Slipping and sliding, like clumsy goats.
Each snowflake whispers, 'Catch me if you dare!'
While squirrels steal snacks without a care.

A penguin slides on a frozen pond,
Belting out tunes, he's truly fond.
His frosty friends form a choir near,
But all we hear is, 'Can you please clear?'

With laughter echoing, snowballs crunched,
Winter’s magic is wildly munched.
In this frosty land of sheer delight,
Where giggles pierce the silent night.

Windows to the Heart of Winter

Through frosted panes we sit and stare,
At a world that seems to give a dare.
A puppy zooms with joy in the freeze,
While a cat just watches, plotting with ease.

Hot cocoa mugs in mittened hands,
With marshmallows bobbing like snowy bands.
Laughter erupts like a snowball fight,
As we watch our pets put on a sight.

Sledding down hills, a wild thrill ride,
With giggles bursting, we just can’t hide.
The snowflakes tumble and play on the air,
Daring us all to join in the flair.

As we warm up by the crackling fire,
Winter’s wonder fuels our desire.
For fun and games in swirling white,
A symphony of joy, a comical sight.

Frosty Silhouettes in Dimming Light

As daylight fades to a soft glow,
The shadows stretch, giving quite a show.
A snowman tiptoes, trying to sneak,
While a hare giggles, feeling chic.

With every gleam of the pale moonlight,
The frosty world asks for a bite.
Snowflakes roll into a round ball,
A game of freeze-tag starts to enthrall.

Twirling and whirling in the cool dusk,
Wearing ice coats, they bask in the musk.
A reindeer prances with quite a flair,
But tumbles down with a frosty scare.

Yet laughter persists in the chilly air,
With joy and cheekiness everywhere.
A world wrapped in winter's playful embrace,
Frosty silhouettes in an endless race.

Silent Frost Echoes

In winter's chill, the snowflakes dance,
They tickle our noses, a frosty romance.
With hats on our heads, we wobble and sway,
Ice slips beneath—catch me if you may!

The penguins giggle as they slide on their bellies,
While we all build castles from snow, like true fellas.
But wait! Was that a snowman trying to flee?
Oh dear, that’s my carrot! Come back to me!

Frozen fingers, we try a hot drink,
Laughing so hard, we can’t even think.
A snowball fight breaks out in the cold,
With laughter and shouts, the memories unfold.

As the sunlight gleams on each frozen shard,
Winter's a circus—oh yes, we applaud!
The frost may be silent, but joy never ends,
In this winter wonderland, playtime transcends!

Glacial Whispers in Twilight

Twilight descends, the world turns to gray,
Snowmen come alive, they gather to play.
One cracks a joke, and oh, what a sight!
As they too fall over, in layers of white.

A yeti appears with a silly grin,
Asks me to join in this cold, mad spin.
We twirl on the ice and tumble with glee,
Creating such chaos, it's most certainly free!

Sledding down hills, we go zooming by,
The laughter erupts, we soar to the sky.
Hot cocoa awaits—let's warm up our toes,
Before the frost bites, and everybody knows!

Each glacial whisper holds tales to retell,
Of snowmen who danced, and that dreaded snowbell.
We might be frozen, but spirits run warm,
In this funny frolic, we weather the storm!

Mirrors of a Frozen Dream

Reflecting the fun, we glide on the glaze,
With shivers and giggles, we're caught in a daze.
An ice slide awaits, let's all take a chance,
Then tumble and roll in this chaotic dance.

Giggles erupt as the ice cracks and splinters,
We break out in song, while the chilly wind splinters.
"More cocoa!" we shout, as we dodge and we weave,
With friends by our side, who'd ever believe?

Dreams are quite funny when frozen in time,
Snowflakes are partners in this silly rhyme.
As we slip and we slide, our shadows take flight,
A festival of laughter glimmers in the night.

Mirrors of frost, reflect all our cheer,
Through frostbitten cheeks, the delight is so near.
In this whimsical world of laughter and beams,
We find inner warmth in our frozen dreams!

Shattered Crystals in Blue Light

Shattered crystals twinkle, like stars in the frost,
We laugh at each other, at all we've lost.
A swirl of excitement in the frosty air,
As snowflakes conspire to tangle our hair.

The squirrels start chattering, trying to bribe,
With acorns of whimsy, in winter's wild tribe.
We chase down the ice with a slip and a spin,
Sharing a giggle, through thick and through thin.

In this frozen ballet, we waltz and we tumble,
Each pirouette ends in a chuckle or crumble.
We gather the warmth from each bright-hearted friend,
In this chill-laden frolic, let the fun never end!

Beneath the blue light, our laughter ignites,
With shattering crystals, our playful ignites.
Through icy adventures, our hearts take to flight,
In joyous assemblies, we revel in light!

Crystalline Thoughts

In a fridge, I found a friend,
A veggie frozen, without an end.
It wore a coat of icy glaze,
In this chilly world, it sways.

My thoughts are trapped in frosty shells,
Like penguins trapped in icy swells.
I drop a joke, it freezes tight,
Teeth chattering, laughing’s a fright.

With each cold breeze, ideas slide,
I ponder where my brilliance hides.
A snowman giggles, forming a grin,
Sipping hot cocoa, where to begin?

So here's to thoughts that chill the heart,
Wrapped in blankets, that's the art.
A frosty muse, playful and bright,
I’ll dance with winter, hold on tight.

The Breath of Winter

Upon the window, frost paints screens,
Little patterns, just like dreams.
I blow on glass and watch it swirl,
A dragon's breath, or is it a pearl?

My nose is red, like a cherry bright,
Wearing layers, oh what a sight!
I trip on snowballs, laughter erupts,
Winter’s clumsiness, just interrupts.

Sledding down hills, I lose control,
Spin like a top, oh how I roll!
My hat flies off, a festive spree,
Chasing it down, I’m filled with glee.

Let’s toast to winter, the season's fun,
As we chase snowflakes, one by one.
With giggles and shivers, we’ll take our stand,
In this frosty land, it’s all quite grand!

Enchanted by Frost

Frosty fairies dance on roofs,
In fluffy slippers, they've lost their hooves.
I join the waltz, but tumble round,
In enchanted chill, my grace is drowned.

Icicles dangle like teeth from above,
I hear them gleefully whisper 'love.'
A slippery patch, what a surprise,
Down I go, in a frosty guise.

The snowflakes giggle as they take flight,
Tickling my nose with pure delight.
Each flake a friend, let's all rejoice,
In this chilly world, we'll raise our voice.

So prance and twirl, let laughter flow,
With winter wonders, let's steal the show.
In frosty realms where joy ignites,
We'll sketch our dreams on snowy nights.

Fleeting Moments in Ice

Moments freeze like popsicles here,
Where laughter echoes, loud and clear.
A slip on ice, I take a dive,
Rolling around, it keeps me alive.

Snowmen gossip, wearing their hats,
Sharing secrets and old-style chats.
I’ll join the fun, with a carrot nose,
Making merry wherever it goes.

Fleeting joys in a winter veil,
Snowball fights and epic tales.
Each laugh a gem, buried in snow,
Moments of joy, don’t let them go.

So skidding and sliding, let’s find our way,
In this chilly dance, we’ll laugh and play.
Each icy chuckle, a memory bright,
In fleeting moments, find pure delight.

Imprisoned in Time

The clock is frozen, tick gone awry,
Penguins in tuxedos dance by and by.
Snowflakes stumble, tripping on air,
Time’s gone on holiday, it just doesn’t care.

Frosty mustaches on snowman faces,
Chill winds whisper through cold, silly places.
A snowball fight turns into a brawl,
With each hurl, a belly laugh and a fall.

The icicles dangle like sharp, big teeth,
While squirrels scurry by, they plot and they breathe.
They gather snow acorns from trees of blue,
In this frosty wonderland, absurdity grew.

So raise a toast with hot cocoa, please,
Cheers to the freeze and its goofy freeze.
Laughter echoes through this chilled out show,
Where time stands still and funny antics flow.

The Quiet Beneath the Frost

Underneath this layer of glistening white,
A rabbit's burrow is cozy and tight.
He's hoarding carrots in a frosty stash,
While snowmen gossip in a waving clash.

Beneath the hush, a snow truck's with glee,
Making jokes with the trees, can you hear the spree?
Snowflakes twirl, with giggles and spins,
While frost bite-tingling dance-offs begin.

In a frozen pond, frogs wear ice skates,
Hopping and slipping, it's fate that awaits.
They launch a ballet that's slapstick and grand,
While the winter owls watch, they roar and they stand.

Here in the stillness, humor runs deep,
The silence bursts forth from shadows we keep.
As each chilly breath fills the air with delight,
We join in the laughter beneath frosty night.

Luminescent Stillness

The moon’s wearing shades, all cool and aloof,
Casting shadows of nonsense, oh what a goof!
Snowflakes shimmer like disco balls bright,
While night critters giggle at the sight.

Furry friends gather, with chitchat and cheer,
Telling tall tales that hang in the air.
Each paw prints a story on the fresh, soft snow,
Where funny mischief and antics can grow.

A haunting howl echoes, it’s laughter, not fright,
As wolves play charades in their frosty moonlight.
They stock up on chuckles like snacks on a plate,
For this joy-filled evening, they can’t wait.

So dance in the stillness, twirl with a friend,
In this luminous landscape, the funny won’t end.
The chill makes us shiver, but laughter stays warm,
In the glow of the night, we weather the charm.

The Heart of Winter's Embrace

Wrapped in blankets like burritos of cheer,
Hot cocoa steaming, winter's nice veneer.
Outside the snowstorms are plotting their fun,
While kittens chase snowflakes, just look at them run!

Sleds shoot down hills like rockets of joy,
Kids squeal with laughter; oh, what a ploy!
The snowman's top hat is askew on his head,
He sighs in defeat as the kids dance instead.

With frosty noses and cheeks blushing red,
Dancing snow angels invade the snowbed.
Each flappy wing leaves a touch of pure glee,
Joy stuck in the flakes, oh look, it's a spree!

When winter wraps tight, with a hug full of mirth,
It spins little stories and laughter gives birth.
Let's toast to the quirks that this season bestows,
In the heart of the freeze, humor sprouts and grows.

The Stillness of Shattered Glass

A mirror cracked but don’t you fret,
The ghosts of winters past are yet.
They dance around in snowflake skirts,
With frozen feet and chilly smirks.

The squirrels in scarves, they take a stand,
While penguins slide, oh isn’t it grand?
The sun pops out, a prankster bright,
While snowmen shiver in sheer delight.

With hiccuping breaths, the icicles chime,
As laughter escapes, oh, what a time!
They'll tell you tales of winter's fuss,
But hold your hot cocoa and hop on the bus!

In frozen glee, we all conspire,
To make snowballs out of icy fire.
The stillness breaks with each silly joke,
In this glassy glimmer, let’s all poke!

Permafrost Dreams

Frosty dreams of a fluffy bed,
But wake up with snowflakes on your head.
The penguins plot a winter parade,
While the snowmen are serenely afraid.

Hot chocolate wishes float through the air,
As marshmallows dance without a care.
Chasing snowflakes, we giggle and tumble,
Then trip on ice and take a big stumble!

In a world where cold is a big joke,
The frozen pastry chef bursts from smoke.
With pastry snowmen and icicle treats,
We'll gobble them up, oh what funny feats!

Yet as the laughter lifts and glows,
There's always someone who stomps on toes.
In permafrost dreams, let's joyfully scheme,
To make winter fun—oh, what a team!

A Frostbitten Dawn

At dawn's arrival, a brrr so grand,
Frosty whiskers on every hand.
The sun is yawning, still half asleep,
While snowflakes giggle and take a leap.

The rabbits wear socks; it’s quite bizarre,
As penguins wonder just where we are.
With floppy boots and hats askew,
We trip on frost, oh what a view!

Carrots for noses and eyes made of coal,
Snowmen unite to form a pole.
With frosty banter and snowball throws,
We laugh till we ache and feel our toes!

As the dawn unveils its chilly grin,
In this frozen playground, let’s dive in!
For what better fun than a frosty cheer,
With laughter echoing far and near?

Shadows Beneath the Snow

Beneath the snow, the shadows play,
A frozen ballet in a frosty way.
With giggles tucked in icy gloves,
They tumble and roll like playful doves.

The owls in top hats sing with flair,
While snowflakes do pirouettes in the air.
Chimneys puff out with a merry tune,
As snowmen wish upon a moon.

The ice is cracked with laughter's might,
While snowball shenanigans take flight.
A cheeky squirrel nicks a mitt,
“Hey, come back here!” we all admit.

So gather ‘round this chilly show,
And join the fun beneath the snow.
We'll dance and twirl till the sun shines bright,
With shadows that giggle in morning light!

Choreography of the Cold

In the frosty realm where penguins glide,
They dance on ice with a comical stride.
With flippers wide, they twirl and spin,
Not a care in the world for the chill or the wind.

Snowflakes waltz in wild disarray,
As squirrels play tag in the icy ballet.
They tumble and slide, a frosty parade,
In this frozen theater, a show well played.

The snowman joins with a carrot nose,
He grooves and shuffles, strikes a pose.
But when he melts, oh, what a sight,
A puddle of giggles in the soft moonlight.

So come and join this winter ball,
With laughter and joy, we'll never fall.
For in the cold, where we can't feel our toes,
We'll dance through the freeze, whatever the woes.

The Memory of a Thaw

Once winter wrapped all in a frosty embrace,
But warm winds whispered of spring’s happy grace.
The icicles dripped in a melodious tune,
As puddles formed little lakes under the moon.

The bears hibernated, dreaming of pies,
While raccoons plotted with mischief and lies.
They woke up confused, looking for snacks,
Only to find fruit carts and sunny tracks.

A thaw turned the snowmen into shy ghosts,
With hats tumbling down, they became playful hosts.
They laughed as they melted, a puddle parade,
Making a splash in the sun’s tender shade.

So let us remember on this journey we take,
That laughter and warmth are the best kind of wake.
For when the cold melts and warmth finds its way,
We’ll dance in the sunshine, come what may.

Reflections Beyond the Frost

Mirrors of ice in the morning light,
Show a world filled with giggles and frostbite.
Polar bears stop to check their own style,
In a comical pose that'll make you smile.

The snowflakes giggle, as they softly fall,
Tickling the noses of creatures small.
A rabbit hops by with a clumsy sway,
It slides and it grins, oh what a display!

Snowball fights break out, a friendly affair,
With snowmen shouting, "Hey, that's not fair!"
The icicles clatter as they join in the fray,
With laughter echoing through the cold winter day.

So take a moment to look at the sights,
The fun in the cold, the amusing delights.
For in every shard of frozen glass,
There's a story of joy that will always last.

Shimmering Veils of Cold

In shimmering veils, the frost takes a bow,
Where penguins giggle, and snowflakes know how.
They twirl and they spark in the winter's embrace,
Dancing with joy, a frosty ballet space.

The snowman's top hat became quite the scene,
As squirrels invade, sneaky and keen.
They pull a few pranks, oh what a delight,
As the snowman chuckles with sheer frozen might.

Hot cocoa flows where the chill can't intrude,
As hot marshmallows bubble, sweetening the mood.
The elves play hopscotch on icy glass floors,
While stories of warmth fill the cold's open doors.

So laugh with the chill and let spirits soar,
In this glistening realm, we'll discover much more.
For among the cold, where the laughter is bold,
Are moments of joy, endless and gold.

Mirrors of Winter

In the mirror, snowflakes dance,
They twirl like they own the chance.
Missed the puddle, slipped and slid,
Oops! The ground was unforbid.

Frosty breath, a puff of fun,
I tried to catch it on the run.
Then it vanished, just like that,
Laughing loudly, 'What a spat!'

A snowman stood with carrot nose,
Said, "I'm cool!" as winter froze.
But I tripped and made him frown,
Guess who's rolling all the way down?

With mittens on, I threw a ball,
It bounced and hit the cat and all.
In the chaos, laughter reigned,
A winter's day that's humor stained.

Silent Crystals

Silent crystals, gleaming bright,
They giggle in the morning light.
Found a snowdrift, leapt with glee,
Landed flatly, oh dear me!

Frosted branches, a silly sight,
Birds wearing hats, what a delight!
One took off, with a chirpy laugh,
Caught my scarf, then did the giraffe!

Ice, it cracks beneath my toes,
Skating sideways, 'Look at those!'
But I twirled and lost my grace,
Now I’m all over the place!

Hot cocoa spills, oops, what a mess!
Wrapped in blankets, I must confess.
That winter charm, so frosty and right,
Turns every blunder into pure delight!

Fragments of Stillness

Fragments of stillness, a snowflake sigh,
I duck and dodge as they float by.
Each flake whispers, 'Catch me if you dare!'
But I slip and slide, my face a glare!

Drawing hearts on the frosty pane,
A gust of wind gives me disdain.
'No art for you!' it shouts with glee,
I guess I'll frost my nose for free!

Penguins waddling, strutting their stuff,
"Hey buddy, is this winter tough?"
I reply, "Just chilling, can't you see?"
While they snicker, I trip on a tree!

Snowball fights go on with might,
But I aimed high, and oh, what a fright!
The snowman grinned as I fell flat,
It seems he was the clever cat!

Frosted Memories

Frosted memories find their way,
Snowflakes like dancers in ballet.
I tried to leap, but tripped and fell,
Now here I lie, with a snowy shell!

A snow angel grinned, 'Look at me!'
But my fluffle turned to comedy.
With arms spread wide, I made my mark,
Till a dog came by, and poof! No spark.

Hot chocolate spills, I squealed with cheer,
Winter’s little mess brings no fear.
Marshmallows float, tiny ships,
Until my cat thinks he can sip!

As snowflakes fall, I stand amazed,
Caught in laughter, I feel so dazed.
With each funny fall, life overlaps,
In frosty moments, joy perhaps!

The Lament of the North Wind

Oh, how I blow and twist about,
With frosty breath and a cheeky shout.
Chasing snowflakes, I take my flight,
But they giggle away, oh, such a fright!

The trees they shiver, dance in place,
As I whirl around with my icy grace.
They call me names, oh, can you believe?
I’m just the wind, I don’t mean to grieve!

The sun will mock as I chide and tease,
A frosty jester who never flees.
I’ll swirl around till my mischief’s done,
Then vanish away with a giggling run.

Yet as I go, here’s the final sting,
You’ll not forget the chill that I bring.
So laugh, dear friends, while I’m in town,
For one day soon, I’ll wear a frown!

Reflections in a Silvered Pool

In a pool so clear, I see my face,
With fish swimming by, oh what a race!
A splash here and there, they give me a wink,
And how do I look? Like a shivering sink!

The reeds dance merrily, waving their heads,
Whispering secrets of what's been said.
"Oh look at him, such a silly sight,"
I chuckle along with the frogs out of fright.

The sun takes a dip, all golden and bold,
While I try to balance, I am quite cold.
Then a plop! A deer jumps right in,
And suddenly, we're both wearing a grin!

Splashing and laughing, we've started a game,
The water reflects, but no one feels shame.
In the ripples of joy, let worries take flight,
Together here, everything's just right!

Veiled Glistening Shadows

The shadows play hide and seek all night,
Glistening in frost, oh what a sight!
Between the trees, they jump and glide,
Making me chuckle at the tricks they hide.

“Oh, is that you, a sneaky old branch?”
I shout to the shadows, give them a chance.
They giggle and wiggle in the pale moonlight,
It’s a game of silliness, pure delight!

Frosty whispers tickle my ear,
“What’s your name?” asks a shadow near.
I tumble and trip in my frosty dance,
A sight to behold, a rather odd chance.

Yet despite all the fun, the dawn starts to break,
The shadows retreat, but I’m wide awake.
With a sigh and a laugh, I bid them adieu,
Till next I see them, oh what will we do?

A Dance of the Frigid Dawn

As dawn arises, a dance on the snow,
The cold nips my toes, but I twirl to and fro.
With frosted breath, I start to prance,
Even the snowflakes join in my dance!

The icicles hang, like twinkling lights,
They jingle and jangle, oh what delights!
“Let’s shimmy, let’s shake, let’s swirl with glee!”
The shivers keep coming, they’re singing with me.

A rabbit jumps in, oh what a feat,
With paws in the air, he can’t find his feet.
We stumble and giggle, a slippery cheer,
While the sun peeks over, our dance rears clear.

So join in the fun, don’t be shy or meek,
Embrace the chill, let your laughter peak.
For the dawn may be frigid, but joy's all around,
In this whimsical waltz, let our spirits abound!

Shadows Cast by Winter’s Touch

The snowmen are grinning, quite wise,
With carrots for noses and chuckling eyes.
They tell the best jokes; oh what a sight,
As they ponder the warmth, with hearts full of light.

Frosty dogs skip with a wagging tail,
Slipping on ice—oh, a comical trail!
They leap and they bound, then land in a heap,
As snowdrifts snicker, their laughter runs deep.

Icicles dangle from houses with glee,
Like frozen performers, they dangle quite free.
They drip and they drop, and each splash does tease,
With a slippery wink, they dance in the breeze.

Penguins in tuxedos, oh what a laugh,
Strutting in style, a marvelous half.
With flippers flapping, they waddle and spin,
Creating a ruckus, a frosty grin!

The Tranquility of Frigid Depths

In a world that's frosty, all covered in white,
Where penguins are skiing and feeling quite bright.
They slide down the slopes with a jubilant cheer,
While snowflakes fall gently, like laughter we hear.

Bubbles in ponds wear a frosty cool hat,
While fish wear their scarves, isn't that where it's at?
They giggle and swim in a shimmering dance,
In this chilly party, they all take a chance.

The trees wear white coats, just like a parade,
With branches like arms waving, they serenade.
Squirrels scamper about, in winter's embrace,
Trying to find nuts while keeping up the pace.

Chill in the air yet the fun won't grow old,
With chattering teeth, they tell tales bold and cold.
Each moment a giggle beneath winter's shroud,
In this frosty wonder, let laughter be loud!

Ethereal Forms in Frosted Stillness

They say every snowflake is special, it’s true,
Just look at their shapes; they’re all quite askew.
The snowmen debate, ‘Is this hat too bright?’
And fall into heaps, what a comical sight!

The rabbits are dressed in their fluffiest coats,
Prancing on hills, telling tales with bold notes.
They hop around, full of mischief and fun,
In a frosty world where their laughter is spun.

The moon peeks down, with a cheeky grin wide,
As shadows dance softly and playfully slide.
In the still of the night, the whispers arise,
In giggles and chuckles, beneath starry skies.

Snowflakes do waltzes, twirling together,
They swirl through the night, like birds of a feather.
With each playful flurry, they make winter sing,
Creating a spectacle, oh what joy they bring!

Glimmers of Light on Chilling Waters

The pond wears a blanket, all glistening blue,
With ducks pretending to dance as they do.
They quack out a tune, with splashes and flair,
All while they're slipping, unaware in mid-air.

Frogs in their wintery hats gather 'round,
To share all their stories where giggles abound.
They leap in the water, a slippery show,
Dripping with laughter, they paddle below.

Reflections are twinkling like stars on the chill,
Where every splatter brings joy, every thrill.
The fishy comedians swim fast for a skit,
As bubbles rise up, oh what a perfect fit!

Bright sunlight dapples the frosty terrain,
While shadows are laughing, they burst out like rain.
In this chilled setting, where humor takes flight,
The glimmers of laughter keep everything light!

Tapestry of Snow

Snowflakes dance like they've got a plan,
Falling from skies, they land with a span.
I tried to catch one, but it slipped away,
Guess it's got better things to do today.

Sledding down hills with giggles and shrieks,
Wobbling like penguins, we're not at our peaks.
Snowmen in hats, with carrot noses wide,
Looking quite dapper, with no place to hide.

Hot cocoa warms us, but spills like a flood,
Sticky and sweet, it's a chocolatey thud.
The snowball fights bring out our inner child,
With laughter and chaos, life's so wild!

As we clamber home with cheeks all aflame,
Dreaming of snowstorms, we'll do it again.
Frosty adventures, we'll never outgrow,
In this tapestry formed by winter's show.

Subzero Reflections

Mirror, mirror on the snowy ground,
Show me my face, but don't make a sound.
It's frozen so solid, I'm scared it might crack,
A reflection of winter's full-on attack.

I tried to walk softly, just one tiny step,
But slipped like a seal on a smooth surface rep.
Down I went flailing, in a flurry of snow,
My dignity lost, but my laughter will grow!

Reflections of warmth in a frostbitten chill,
Wondering if penguins have mastered this thrill.
My cheeks are a shade that you'll never believe,
I'm the rosy joker, who never will leave!

Underneath all this, the chill can't defeat,
A heart that is beating with life and a beat.
So bring on the frosty, the funny, the bright,
In subzero nights, we'll be all right!

The Pulse of a Frozen Heart

Once a heart was frozen, it had no beat,
Chillin' all day in the snow and the sleet.
But then came a laugh, as bright as a star,
Frost started melting, it didn't go far.

Tick tock went the clock, but the heart didn't know,
Winter gave way, and it started to glow.
With each little chuckle, the pulse found its way,
Sending out warmth in a jocular play!

Ice cubes in my drink that thought they were grand,
Sailed on a sea made of snowflakes and sand.
But with laughter erupting, they lost all their fight,
Froze into puddles while we danced in delight.

So here's to the heart that defrosted by joy,
Bringing out smiles like a snow-covered toy.
The pulse of this laughter shall never depart,
In the humor of winters, we'll stay off the chart!

Still Waters in the Cold Dawn

Morning light dances on surfaces still,
Whispering secrets that send chills down the hill.
A stillness so funny, it couldn't be real,
Like nature's great jest, what's the big deal?

I tripped on a twig, that laughed as I fell,
Echoes of winter, in laughter they dwell.
Reflections of mischief in puddles that freeze,
Let's blame it on dawn, let's all have a tease!

Snow angling sideways, like it's checking its style,
With coats on the rack, they are not worth the while.
Fumbling and tumbling in boots far too large,
Yet we head to the fun without any charge.

So let's raise a glass to still mornings ahead,
With warmth in our hearts, and laughter to spread.
In these cold, frosty waters, we'll find our glee,
For winter's a joke, and we're the marquee!

Captive Light

In a frozen jar, I caught a star,
It blinked and laughed, oh how bizarre!
It twirled and danced upon the shelf,
Claiming it just wanted to be itself.

But winter’s chill would steal the show,
It turned to ice, and then to glow.
"Let me out!" it giggled with glee,
While I just sipped my warm cup of tea.

I opened wide the icy lid,
And out it shot, like a playful kid.
Now it flits about, but with a twist,
It tells me jokes, oh how I’ve missed!

So here we are, a curious pair,
A warming drink and a spark of flair.
In frigid air, we'll laugh all night,
And capture more of that fleeting light.

Ghosts of the Unseen

Through frosty glass, I peek and pry,
The ghosts of winter laugh and sigh.
Their scarves wrapped tight, they sway with flair,
Tickling my nose, with chilly air!

They dance on rooftops, a jolly sight,
Challenging me to join their flight.
I shiver, giggle, and shake my fist,
"You can’t catch me! I'm a winter wisp!"

One ghost, so bold, took off his hat,
Swirled in snowflakes, like a playful cat.
"You can't unsee us—join the fun!"
But all I want is to warm in the sun.

So off they float, those merry sprites,
While I chase comfort on chilly nights.
I wave goodbye as they glide away,
The ghosts of winter, come back to play!

Shards of Winter Light

In shards of glass, I see the sun,
Reflecting laughter, oh what fun!
They split and scatter on my floor,
Like little clowns at a frosty door.

I stomp my feet, they scatter ‘round,
With giggles echoing all around.
"Keep up, you shards! I’ll catch you next!"
But they just laugh, oh, how vexed!

With every step, a rain of bright,
They twinkle out, just out of sight.
I tumble, roll, and ache to find,
Those merry fragments that tease the mind.

But soon I spot a gleaming piece,
That makes my heart and laughter increase.
"Caught ya now!" I beam with pride,
As winter’s trickery hits full stride.

Ethereal Frost

On my window, frost paints a tale,
Of funny shapes with a shivery trail.
A penguin winks, and a snowman grins,
As winter's mischief begins to spin.

With each chilly breath, they come alive,
Planning antics, oh how they strive!
"Let's throw a party, a frosty spree!"
While I just chuckle, sipping my tea.

They leap and jiggle, a frosty crew,
With flip-flops on, they dance and woo.
"Don't slip!" I warn with a playful shout,
But they just giggle and spin about.

As dawn appears, the magic fades,
But winter's laughter stays in cascades.
I'll wait for night, for their tricks in frost,
For each chilly moment is never lost!

A Symphony of Cold Shadows

In winter's grip, a squirrel slips,
He dances 'round on frozen tips.
With every leap, he looks askance,
A slip and slide — his frosty dance.

The snowflakes swirl like little stars,
While penguins plot their funny cars.
A snowman sings a jolly tune,
His carrot nose just lost its boon.

The icicles glimmer, sharp and bright,
As snowmen chase the chill of night.
A blizzard plays a lively song,
But finds its notes just all gone wrong.

So here we laugh at chilly whims,
At frosty fumbles, slips, and grins.
For even in this cold embrace,
A little fun makes winter a chase.

Unraveled Threads of Frosted Silence

A scarf unwinds from chilly necks,
While tea spills over, who'd expect?
The kettle whistles out a tune,
As saucers dance, a frosty swoon.

The penguin waddles, oh so proud,
He trips on ice, then bows to crowd.
An elder bear with clumsy grace,
Decides to join the frigid race.

Snowflakes land on noses, bright,
In winter’s grip, they start a fight.
With laughter ringing through the air,
The muffs all chuckle, quite a flair.

And though the world grows white and cold,
These threads of joy are still retold,
As smiles shine through the frosted gloom,
In silly tales, the chill finds room.

The Lament of a Crystal Heart

A heart of ice begins to melt,
With every joke, the warmth is felt.
Yet penguins in their tuxedoes fair,
Complain of cold and well, despair!

Their flippers flail in comic streaks,
As snowflakes spin in funny peaks.
The gopher pops from out of snow,
To see the frozen, silly show.

A heart once blue now laughs aloud,
At frosty slips and joys unbowed.
For laughter’s warmth will surely thaw,
The icy grip of winter's claw.

So here's to hearts that dare to smile,
To chilly jokes that stretch a mile.
We'll dance amid the frosty cheer,
As laughter echoes, loud and clear.

Frigid Mists and Untold Stories

In mists so thick, a snowball flies,
Turns out it’s just a hound in disguise.
The trees all shiver in delight,
As frosty clouds inspire a fight.

A squirrel plots a grand retake,
With nutty schemes for winter’s sake.
Yet slips down hard into the snow,
And giggles stand where chills do grow.

The frozen pond, a mirror bright,
Reflects the laughs and goofy sights.
With ice skates rank, they take a chance,
To glide and swirl in winter's dance.

These frigid mists bring tales anew,
Of laughter's warmth and playful blue.
For even in the chill we find,
A treasure trove of laughs entwined.

Milton Keynes UK
Ingram Content Group UK Ltd.
UKHW022340171124
451242UK00007B/72

9 789916 944745

An Aspiring Au... n
Of An Auth...
Publication

John Roberts

An Aspiring Author's Articulation Of An Author's Journey To Publication

With so much information flooding the internet these days, it's often difficult for aspiring writers to know where to start and what advice they should take.

Falling victim to this madness, I began writing a blog on Substack where I shared my own experiences of becoming an author and gave my own take on issues that I encountered along the way.

None of the blogs featured here are meant to be 100% accurate. This is just my own interpretation of subjects that cropped up in my author journey across 2023 and 2024.

To find out more about the blogs and the various writing projects I have going on, please visit www.CorneliusCone.co.uk[1]

1. http://www.corneliuscone.co.uk

JOHN ROBERTS

John Roberts was born in a small market town called Banbury in the UK. In 1999, he moved to Southampton where he now lives with his wife and son. He has been a freelance writer since 2008 with varied success, a long suffering Newcastle United FC supporter, Formula 1 fanatic and works the night shift at a local supermarket.

John is the author of the adult crime thriller series; The Blake Langford Adventures. Blake works for Special Branch in London and alongside his team of agents, he battles his own personal battles as well as those potentially threatening the British Government in sometimes, unorthodox fashion, however, family is always his main focus as he fights for his country.

John Roberts is also the author of the children's series; Bennie Barrier's Big City Adventures and co-author of the children's adventure series, "The New Adventures Of Cornelius Cone And Friends" with his friend, Steve Boyce. All of these adventures can be found on Amazon Kindle and in most well known book shops worldwide.

JOHN'S BLOGS

Introduction

INTRODUCTION

If you've read this far, I thank you and I appreciate you dearly.
For those of you who are aspiring to become published authors in the near future, I hope these pages can help provide some kind of inspiration to your journey along the way.
My name is John Roberts, I am a self published author from The New Forest on England's south coast.
Ever since childhood, I have enjoyed exploring other worlds and going on magical journeys with my writing as a form of escapism from the trials and tribulations of the modern world.
Throughout this book, you will encounter a year of blog posts from my Substack Blog as I continue to progress through my writing journey.
A lot of the information here is my own personal opinion on things. It is by no means 100% accurate and you should always do your research before embarking on your own writing projects. This book is sharing some light relief that us writers often need.
If you'd like to reach out to me at any time, you can catch me at JohnRobertsAuthor.Substack.com
Until next time, write on.
JR

Hmm, So This Is New...

Hello Substack world,

This is a medley of some of my hints, tips, observations, general screw-ups and light conversation and I hope you gain some inspiration, or at least some amusement, from reading it.

I'm John Roberts, the author of the crime fiction series; The Blake Langford Adventures, author of the new Children's series; Bennie Barrier's Big City Adventures and co-author of The New Adventures Of Cornelius Cone And Friends with my friend, Steve Boyce.

My newsletter is a regular ramble about writing, publishing, my inspirations, challenges, opportunities and my overall journey to being an author today. I'd love to hear from you all and I'll answer as many questions as I can. Feel free to follow me on Facebook, TikTok and Twitter and I'll share as many of your posts as I can. This whole experiment is a two way thing so interaction from you makes this newsletter a whole lot more interesting than just my general ramblings.

So, how did I start on my writing journey? I'm heading all the way back to the 1980's when I was in Primary School in a small market town called Banbury in the UK.

You've heard the nursery rhyme, unfortunately Banbury Cross is just a glorified roundabout in the centre of town but it definitely has a quirkiness about it.

Anyway, in Primary School, my teacher at the time, started a writer's workshop. This allowed all of the class to explore our imagination and write some fantastical stories about some far away lands. (Believe me, when you're in a country that has rain most of the year, any far flung, sun drenched oasis is paradise!)

At the end of the day, the teacher would read out somebody's story to the class after each writing session. Just seeing the smiles, hearing the laughter and experiencing the joy that storytelling could bring to people, even at that young age, stuck with me for life.

We all have our own version of the world that we live in. Some of us are more fortunate than others but wealth should not be measured simply by money or possessions. Whatever problems, challenges or difficulties people face, even if you're having a really bad day, allowing yourself a few minutes of escapism in a good book can truly save lives.

As our lives become ever busier, the advance of AI and the internet meaning that we are experiencing information overload. Choosing what and how we consume information is more important than ever. From a mental health point of view as well as physical health, we need to make time to slow down. Time to take a breath and get lost in the amazing fantasy world dreamt up by the talented pool of authors who paint pictures with words across the printed page or screen.

I hope this first venture into the world of Substack has piqued your interest and you'll join me for some more ramblings very soon. Until next time, write on.

JR

Building A New Adventure...

So you came back... that's great. I often get asked what made you start writing?

Besides the inspiration I had from school, I'd always enjoyed the escapism of adventure books and films. The James Bond or Jack Reacher stories where one man travels the world and makes a difference to people's lives. This led to the inspiration for my latest adult crime fiction series; The Blake Langford Adventures. The original Blake adventure, Where No I One Stands Alone, had its first draft written in 2007. Before that time, I'd never really fully committed myself to any kind of worthwhile writing project. Then, in the summer of '07, I had just come out of a long term relationship and found myself with extra time on my hands. Living in The New Forest, we have an amazing coastline nearby so I took a couple of notebooks with me and sat on the beach at Lepe and began noting down some ideas for a novel.

Those ideas sprang into a relationship triangle between Blake, Paula and Rachael as I tried to work out my own emotions and feelings after a break-up and that played into the role that Blake finds himself in. He still holds on to the love he had for Rachael but it is always just out of reach.

I wrote the first draft and several edits of Where No One Stands Alone over the following year or so before storing it away in a filing cabinet (remember those?) and forgetting about it for many years.

In 2018, my friend Steve Boyce, created a children's series called Cornelius Cone And Friends. Being a father myself, the original story piqued my interest and I suggested a few further storylines that he could pursue in the series. To my surprise, Steve offered me the chance to create my own take on the series which has so far spawned 80 ebook adventures as well as 14 compilation paperbacks.

Suddenly, my passion for writing had returned and even though I'd never originally considered myself as a children's author, I was able to focus on that and see the world through the eyes of my 4 year old child at the time. What interested him? What magical adventures and how can the imagination of a child see the uniqueness of the world around us that, as adults, we tend to miss. An imagination where everything around us is alive. The plants, the roadside cones and barrier, a shopping trolley, a wet floor cone, a bus, a wheel clamp, a bin, what if they could all talk and interact with humans? What if they could have their own little community of friendships, relationships and even betrayal and deceit. What lessons could children learn from how these characters interacted and reacted? The list was endless and it opened up a whole new world of discovery.

This became the basis of building new adventures. What could a humble traffic cone who works in a Maintenance Yard on the edge of The New Forest do to make his world come alive? He could go to work daily and stand in line to make sure that the workers are safe from vehicles driving by. But that would only be half of the story. As adults, we tend to fall into a work, sleep, work, sleep, pattern that eventually leads us towards burnout and depression. Children view the world differently. There needs to be time to play. Time to explore. Time to enjoy conversations with your best friends. To tell jokes. Be competitive. Make a difference. This is where Cornelius Cone leads their imaginations including 4 Christmas specials where Cornelius Cone makes sure that Santa can get all of the presents to all of the children in time for Christmas Day.

If you can find a way to tap into that imagination and include things that make the story feel real to the children who read it, you have a great platform to build your adventure on!

Catch up with me in the next newsletter as I discuss the effect of the pandemic, how Cornelius Cone found popularity in schools and how Blake Langford was finally published. Until next time, write on.

JR

The Pandemic And A New Dream Realised...

Ah yes, 2020, the start of a new decade, a new focus, a year of productivity, well we all know how that turned out. Surprisingly, the lockdowns of 2020 led to my most creative output that I've had in many years.

I'd begun writing alongside my friend, Steve Boyce, a collection of short stories that became The New Adventures Of Cornelius Cone And Friends series but I felt that I needed to refocus on adult fiction again. After sorting through some old paperwork, I discovered the first draft of Where No One Stands Alone which I had written in 2007.

As with all first drafts, it was rough with more holes than the average UK road but it reignited my interest in writing again. After having relatively strong sales with my Children's books, it gave me the confidence to try again at cracking the adult fiction market.

I learnt very quickly that quality over quantity is the way to go and I ruthlessly edited 120,000 words down to around 80,000 words. Making every word count and every interaction mean something to the final outcome was key.

Growing up, I'd always enjoyed adventure stories in far away places that as a child, I often dreamed about and now I had the chance to take Blake there and put him in situations where he had to rely on his own initiative to survive. I didn't want him to be a superhero. The Marvel franchise has saturated that market already. But I wanted to give him a human feel. The kind of guy you'd meet in the pub. Show his strong, aggressive, determined side whilst also encapsulating his vulnerability and his emotional journey too.

We've all been in a situation where our love for someone has led us to make bad decisions. Blake has to find a way to look at things objectively whilst also battling the needs of his own relationships, especially after learning that he has an 8 year old son.

Where No One Stands Alone was finally released in 2022 to a positive reaction amongst readers. Finding myself in a completely different writing niche gave me freedom to express things in the Blake Langford series that I couldn't pursue as a children's author. Following feedback from readers, I began considering a series of Blake Langford adventures which led to the 2023 release of the second novel, Underneath The Covers.

From the enthusiastic child who felt recognition at school when the teacher read out my short story to the class, through the years to rediscovering my writing passion after a relationship break-up and the subsequent great reset that Covid gave us; I've learnt that there is no linear path to becoming an author.

Turning 40 in 2022, my years of friendships, relationships and general life experiences seem to find their way into my writing. I always have my notes app ready to jot down any snippets that I hear in conversation or whenever inspiration strikes. I can almost guarantee that without making a physical note, these ideas seem to just disappear.

You play an important role in the movie of your life and when the stage is set for you to shine, you need to have the courage to stand in the spotlight and make your mark on this world. As a good friend once told me, only I can tell my story my way and you never know who is reading or how you will impact their lives.

Until next time, write on.

JR

Writer's Block And A World Of Your Imagination

Life tends to throw challenges our way all the time. Some of them we rise up to, others take a little longer to resolve. In a world where mental health issues are becoming more and more recognised, finding time to take a breath, step aside from the realities and struggles in life can often be a great tool for finding your way out of a dark space.

The same is true in fiction writing. I find it an incredible escape into the world of Blake Langford or Cornelius Cone where nothing is impossible. The daily gripes, although needed to make fiction realistic, seem to take on a third party feeling. Problems you are working through in day-to-day life can be placed upon your characters and feel less personal to yourself. When faced with a difficult decision, reframing it into, how would X deal with this can create a surprising new perspective on things.

A lot of people ask how do I deal with writer's block? We've all had those days when the words won't flow no matter what we try. So I have what I call a scribble book. I allow myself 30 minutes to just write in my scribble book. It doesn't matter what it is. If it doesn't make any sense. If it's a rant or just random words on a page. Just getting the words written down seems to declutter my mind. If, after 30 minutes, the words still don't flow then I put it all aside and try again later. But 9 times out of 10, it works. I liken it to going into somebody's attic. You have years and years of material things that you have kept just in case it's needed. Boxes upon boxes of clutter. Slowly, you remove each box and decide whether it's really worth keeping or not. That's the job of my scribble book, it slowly removes the clutter from my mind, piece by piece until it finds the inspiration it's looking for. Try it, I'd love to hear your experiences with it.

Recently, I have taken on a new project involving one of the main characters from the Cornelius Cone series, Bennie Barrier. After over 80 adventures with Cornelius Cone, I felt like it was time to pursue a different direction. Steve Boyce, my co-author for the Cornelius Cone series, is currently working on his third animated children's book for the series so it felt like a good time for me to pivot into a new direction.

From reading the stories with children, a lot of the feedback was asking for minor characters to have their own storyline. This led to me writing Bennie Barrier's Big City Adventures. The plan so far is for at least 12 new adventures with Bennie Barrier as the lead character, as he leaves Cornelius Cone's Maintenance Team behind and moves into Southampton City Centre. Introducing new friends and enemies into Bennie's life leads him into all kinds of situations in which he needs to use the lessons that he learnt with Cornelius to survive. Some of the new ebooks for this series are already available and there will be a compilation of the new Bennie Barrier's Big City Adventures in 2024.

Looking at the world around us through a child's eyes can give you a whole new perspective on situations and ideas. Snippets of information and situations that you find yourself in can hide a mountain of clues for future storylines. For example, in my previous job, we had an older man in the team who always misheard people or pretended to mishear you just to make you laugh. He led me to create Grandad Cone who has the same characteristics as my colleague in the Cornelius Cone adventures. Likewise, Bertie Bin's belching and farting is also based on another colleague who takes great pleasure in telling everyone that it's "better out than in," enough said.

So I guess my tip for honing your imagination and to try and avoid a writing block is to be curious. Make notes about everything you see and hear. You never know when that little snippet of information will pay you back in the future.

Until next time, write on.

JR

If I Only Had Time... Welcome To The Excuses Market

We've all been there haven't we? "I just don't have the time to write..." "I don't have the money to follow my dream..."

I guess the big question is what does success look like to you? We're all different. Some people would just like to be healthy. Some people think that being a millionaire would fix everything. Excuses become our daily ritual that, if spoken often enough, becomes our reality. If you're constantly talking negatively to yourself, how are you ever going to have the confidence to challenge yourself and achieve something extraordinary?

The busy streets of London are vastly different to the picturesque beaches of the Greek islands. The angry, depressed, steely focused glare of someone from the city can evaporate in the Mediterranean sun given the right circumstances. A lot of our limitations live in our own minds. We are the only limiting factor to success. Whether we are the stern focused Londoner or the one walking down the beach with grains of sand between our toes, our environment and the external forces around us dictate our feelings, emotions and how we present ourselves.

I've had some friends say they want to write a novel or even their life story, yet they haven't even written the first paragraph.

We all have responsibilities and demands on our time but how much time do we waste on a daily basis. Checking emails, posting on Facebook, scrolling on TwitterX or uploading our life highlights on Instagram? The average person loses up to 3 hours per day scrolling social media. What's stopping you from taking 30 minutes off of social media and focusing on your writing or whatever project you want to pursue? When you feel the urge to pick up the phone, pick up a pen instead. The fear of missing out is turning everyone into mobile phone zombies. This was particularly highlighted in a recent holiday that I had in Rhodes.

10 days with my family on a sun-soaked Greek Island with beautiful beaches, waterparks, historical ruins and amazing traditional

Greek Tavernas. Yet, people in the water parks, on the beaches and in the swimming pools had their phones in plastic bags so they could post live videos on social media rather than seeing what was directly in front of them. Their children playing, people laughing and playing, swimming in the pools, children squealing in delight as they slid down the water slides. But social media was more important than all of those things to a surprising number of people. Children would ask their parents a question but we're ignored because they were too focused on their phones. What kind of world are we heading into and creating for our children?

This is where we come to the excuses market. We are all in control of how we show up in this world and what we do. We have the gift of free will so why would we willingly give this up to the trolls of clicks, likes and hearts over our family?

For years, I said that I wanted to write an adventure novel similar to the James Bond and Jack Reacher adventures that I had grown up reading and watching on TV. In 2007, I started the process but it took until 2021 for the novel to be published. I was guilty of falling into the internet trap and it seems like the addiction to social media is getting worse.

We all hold the key to whether or not our work can make a difference in the future. What we prioritise will make a difference for what we achieve so what's stopping you from doing something amazing?

Until next time, write on.

JR

The Trouble With Later

We're all guilty of it aren't we? Oh, I'll do it later. I'll call them later. The trouble is we're living a life where we don't believe that we will die. That we have infinite time until suddenly, the reality of life hits us and we're left to pick up the pieces left behind.

Controversial? Let me explain. As a child, I always enjoyed writing and often wrote stories for my parents and school teachers to read. I see the same enthusiasm in my son today as he proudly shows off the 15 pages he has written about a fantasy world from his own imagination.

Through my teenage years, I encountered a lot of deaths in my family and it began shaping me as an adult years later to not let complacency get in the way of doing what I wanted to do; within reason. Yet, even with this determination, it took the pandemic in 2020 for me to realise that I needed to take my writing ambition seriously or I would forever regret at least not trying to follow my dream.

Those who died today had plans for this evening. Their later never came so whenever I feel like I need to put things off until later, I question the reason why? Am I being lazy? Is the task not high enough on my priority list and if not, does it even need to be done at all?

I had this conversation with a friend a while ago and to put our daily struggles and our procrastination into context; in a hundred years from now, we will all be buried with our relatives and friends. All of our possessions and time spent arguing and putting off our joy will be meaningless. Strangers will live in our homes. Our cars will most likely be scrap metal and our grandchildren or great-grandchildren will hardly know us. At the end of the day, all that will be left behind is a photo in somebody's drawer collecting dust until eventually, that photo fades away too.

Some may argue with the rise of A.I. and the internet that in some digital context we will live forever, yet we tend to forget that we are all just part of a catalogue of millions of social media profiles, authors or statistics on a census.

Doing things later really means that you do not value the task or person in question. Taking the leap of faith that everything will work out as it should can be the difference between being productive and procrastinating. When you're laying on your own death bed, would you rather reflect on your life as an amazing ride where you followed your heart, took risks and made the most of everyday? Or will it be a moment of self reflection and regret for not taking the chance when it was available to you?

Nobody dies wondering how many likes this status will get on social media. Don't let later become never. Trust yourself and make amazing things happen. You are the author of your own story. Make it a good one.

Until next time, write on.

JR

Who is Cornelius Cone?

Back in 2018, my friend, Steve Boyce, created a children's book called Cornelius Cone And Friends. It proved to be very popular and my son enjoyed the storyline so much that he wanted to discover more about Cornelius and his fantasy world.

After discussing ideas with Steve, he encouraged me to join him in writing some new adventures and from that, we now have over 80 ebooks of The New Adventures Of Cornelius Cone available to buy through Amazon. But who is Cornelius Cone?

Steve and I both worked together as postmen in a small village called Hythe which is situated next to The New Forest National Park on the south coast of England. With continuous developments in the area, roadworks seemed to be endlessly causing tailbacks on the local roads and with that came the idea of what if that traffic cone had his own adventure? What if all the other cones and barriers that were situated alongside the cone were actually friends or relatives. This then led to other ideas such as visiting the supermarket. What would a shopping visit look like from the point of view of the shopping trolley or the wet floor cone?

Add into the mix some of the local characters that we engaged with in daily life such as Postman Pete, Mr Mullet, the less than honest shopkeeper, Dave, the head of the maintenance team as well as less obvious characters such as the park bins, Bertie, Bella and Rita Red Bin and you soon begin to create a little community who often get themselves into amusing and somewhat confusing situations.

Each individual character then began resembling people we encountered in daily life too. A man from our local area had a habit of belching and farting loudly in public and generally had poor hygiene so this became the ideal character trait for Bertie Bin. One of our colleagues often came into the office calling out "What's happening then?" and when you told him, he often pretended to be confused with what you had said to him. This gave us the idea for Grandad Cone who was hard of hearing but also very mischievous. Taking ideas from real life situations and people enabled us to make the fantasy characters have a realistic feel to them.

When I was a child, I always enjoyed writing stories and creating my own worlds and during the chaos of the lockdowns in 2020 during the pandemic, Cornelius Cone was a great distraction. I could disappear into his little world where anything was possible. He could compete in a triathlon to raise money for charity. Stop a shady entrepreneur from ripping off the supermarket manager. Take advice from Postman Pete about only driving cars and vans made on a Wednesday because it was the only day the manufacturers and builders were completely focused on the job of making the best vehicles they could. Or just sitting down with his friend Bennie Barrier to have a deep and meaningful conversation about mental health. The possibilities are endless; and with a Bennie Barrier series now complementing the Cornelius Cone story, the series continues to go from strength to strength.

If you'd like to find out more about Cornelius Cone, follow the links below;

The Whole Cone: The Adventures Of Cornelius Cone And Friends Based On The Characters Created By Steve Boyce And John Roberts (The New Adventures Of Cornelius Cone And Friends) https://amzn.eu/d/dqlFlYA

The New Adventures Of Cornelius Cone And Friends: The Whole Cone 2 - Above The High Visibility Belt https://amzn.eu/d/5v8Xpoi

Until next time, write on.

JR

Who is Blake Langford?

Blake Langford, you may have heard the name, you may have read the series of novels but who is he?

Growing up I used to love adventure stories such as the Jack Reacher novels and Ian Fleming's original James Bond stories before they were later made into movies. They depicted a character who was far from perfect. He had his own opinion. His own flaws. And most importantly, he had a gritty realism to his character.

As much as I enjoy sci-fi and other genres, I didn't want to remake Superman or any of the Marvel characters, I wanted to create the character of a middle-aged man in the kind of stories that I would want to read.

So, Blake Langford arrived. Finding a love of writing in school led me to pursue writing a crime novel for many years. After a long term relationship ended in 2007, I found myself with extra time on my hands as I worked through the motions of being single again. I sat on Lepe Beach which is on the south coast of England with a notepad and pen and looked out at the waves of the sea. There is an old house on top of the cliff that overlooks the beach and it gave me the inspiration to use that house as Blake's holiday home when he wasn't working in London. A place to get away from everything. Somewhere to relax and refocus. I guess that was what I was trying to do when I started writing the first novel too.

Gradually, the story which became the first adventure; "Where No One Stands Alone," built up in my mind and the first draft was written in just over three months. I never really gave the idea of being an author another thought for several years until I began co-writing the new Cornelius Cone adventures alongside my friend, Steve Boyce

Becoming a father and the effects of the lockdowns during the pandemic led me to stop making excuses for why I couldn't pursue a writing career. I'd always said that I didn't have the time, yet I would mindlessly lose hours scrolling social media or watching videos.

Channelling that time into constructive writing not only delivered the opportunity to write the Blake Langford and Cornelius Cone stories, it also gave me a sense of fulfilment and joy. They say, if you do something that you love you'll never work a day in your life and that's true with my writing.

So, after many years, I found the original handwritten and typed first draft of "Where No One Stands Alone" in the drawer and began to read through what was written back in 2007. Of course, a lot of the material needed work doing to it, but the essence of the story is still the same. If you had one chance to make amends with the love of your life, would you take it? That was Blake's dilemma. He had emotionally closed off his feelings for Rachael and tried to move on with his life. Then eight years later, Paula, Rachael's sister, arrives to tell him that she is in trouble and needs his help. Blake's need for answers sends him on a personal mission into America and Mexico to find out what really happened when Rachael disappeared.

After receiving positive feedback for the first novel, my family and I flew up to Edinburgh for a long weekend visiting the sights and of course, Holyrood Palace and Edinburgh Castle and dungeons. This triggered an idea of how would Blake react if he was here? What shady side of the Scottish capital could I create to bring Special Branch and Blake to Scotland? I was scratching around for ideas until later that same year, I watched the fireworks on TV on New Year's Eve which showed the Hogmanay Celebrations in Edinburgh. What better cover for a murder and a kidnapping under the cover of fireworks and drunken celebration. Blake was still reeling from how things worked out with Rachael and this would be an ideal time to begrudgingly bring him back into work again and this led to "Underneath The Covers" uncovering the underbelly of city life with a Scottish touch.

If I was to sum up Blake in a few words, I think he would be determined, occasionally reckless, family orientated but fully aware of his flaws. This will become more apparent in the new adventure, "In The Shadow Of My Life" but I won't leave any spoilers here.

Until next time, write on.

JR

What Does It Take To Write A Story?

I often get asked this question. Storytelling has been part of human communication for many generations. Even before the books that we know today were even thought of, groups of people would gather around campfires to share ghost stories and folk tales of yesteryear. The ancient Egyptians even scribed them onto the wall. So what does it take to write a story?

Many of the best stories are based, or at least partly based, on true events with some artistic licence thrown in for dramatic effect. The characters in my children's books are often taken from the characteristics and sayings that people around me use on a daily basis. Making people and places seem real can often be easily achieved by making them about real life.

What we fail to realise, especially with the rise of artificial intelligence, is that we are in fact writing our own stories online for the world to see. That Facebook post which shows you at the beach with family and friends. That Instagram post that shows you enjoying a meal at an Italian restaurant. That song by Elvis Presley that you listened to on Spotify. That Twitter or X post that shows you meeting a celebrity at a nightclub. You've just written the story that John Smith has gone to the beach with his wife Jane, his son Mason, his daughter Emily, he enjoyed Risotto for dinner, that you are a fan of Elvis Presley and you met with an A-list celebrity whilst dancing the night away at the Java Club. See how easy we are making it for AI to build up millions of stories about every single one of us. You can do this too.

So this is how I build up a character profile when writing a story. The first question tends to be, are they an essential part of the plot or are they just background noise. If they're not a stepping stone from one scene to the next scene then they are rejected and the story runs in a different way. From reading crime novels for many years, I tend to write my novels like a puzzle. There are usually three or four stories simultaneously happening to build up to the climax of the novel. In the Blake Langford adventures for example, it is told from multiple viewpoints. In "Where No One Stands Alone," the viewpoints are firstly from Blake, then Rachael, then the Turner Family in Miami and finally Jason Price and his team from the CIA. In building these four worlds and letting them cross over and occasionally clash slowly builds a picture that ends up being the final showdown at the end of the novel. Like building a puzzle, you build the edge first and then slowly work on the prominent features of the picture before drilling down into the final few details to complete it.

Dialogue can be fun too. Whether writing for children's books or adult fiction, everyone enjoys overhearing a good argument or a humorous anecdote from someone. A lot of times we experience confrontations in life or witness it happening on TV. Having dialogue that really crackles as you write it can be a dream for the author. If I'm not sure if the dialogue will flow or fit well in the story, I occasionally ask someone to read the lines of the protagonist with me as the antagonist and by reading the exchange aloud, you can easily hear whether the exchange will work or if it's too scripted or stilted.

I guess my biggest takeaway from this newsletter is, if you want to write a story, first you must stop, listen and observe. See what is happening around you and make notes. Be curious around new people. What are their habits, their traits. Do they have a catchphrase that they always use? Also, take a look at social media. There are literally millions of stories waiting to be discovered there. Oh, Amy went to London and got caught up in the train strikes. How, where, why, when? What could Amy's story be? You want to base a story in London? Go visit it. Take the tube, see the sights, explore areas of London that you wouldn't necessarily find on a tourist brochure. The world is awash with ideas and inspiration. Do you have the spark to ignite it within you? Take a notebook or use an app on your phone, you never know when something extraordinary might pique your imagination.

Until next time, write on.

JR

NaNoWriMo: What Is It And How Can It Work For Me?

Every November, budding writers around the world tackle the annual tradition of NaNoWriMo. Some of you may ask, what on earth is that?

NaNoWriMo is an abbreviation of National Novel Writing Month where people who have had a desire to write a novel but have never had the chance to put pen to paper, commit to writing X amount of words everyday throughout the month of November. No editing, just free flowing writing for an entire month in the hope that by the end of the month, they will have around 30,000 words which will represent a significant part of a novel.

But why do they do it? And does it work? Let's dig in a little deeper. Generally, it is accepted that you need to do something consistently for 28 days to form a habit. That is what this is. You are forming a habit of writing, say for example, from 8pm to 9pm every day for a month or perhaps 2,000 words per day, every day for a month. By doing this consistently, you are arming your brain to believe that you can do the task in hand, consistently, and are achieving results. Where before the TV, social media or other distractions would take up your time, you are making a conscious effort to allow yourself the time to do what you enjoy, write. But does it work? Am I just going to scribble a load of rubbish and then look back at the end of the month on a pile of paperwork that I'd rather set on fire than publish? Well, perhaps. But before we go down that route, let's talk about intention and the role our unconscious mind plays in this.

Whenever you read a novel by your favourite author, you rarely read the entire novel in one sitting. You may read a few chapters each night before bed or on your lunch break at work and then put it down for a while to sleep or carry on with day-to-day life. When you return to that novel, within a couple of paragraphs, your subconscious mind has picked up where you left the story from the last time that you read it. Almost as if you had paused the DVD of your life, the mind manages to put the pieces together so by the end of reading that novel, you have a very strong understanding of what it was about. This is similar to how NaNoWriMo can help you kick start that project that you have had in the back of your mind. You are frequently revisiting the same material. Like reading a novel, your story line is taking you with it on the adventure. You are the captain of the ship and it's up to you whether you take it into choppy waters or calm seas.

So what happens if I hit a writing block during NaNoWriMo? It happens to us all. We decide at 8pm that we are going to sit down and write for an hour. Throughout the day, we've had several amazing ideas that are going to turn our writing into the next Lord Of The Rings trilogy, we sit down to write and then.... Nothing. Not a single word or idea comes to mind. As I discussed in a previous newsletter, I have my own scribble book which is literally a cheap little notebook from the local newsagents. When I have that dreaded block, I take out this book and write. Just write anything that's on your mind. Unpack everything. Swear. Argue. Express everything that's bothering you from the day. That person annoyed you. You wish that person noticed you. You want to kill your boss. Whatever it is. Even if it makes absolutely no sense, get it written out in that scribble book. Believe it or not, when you have scribbled down all of the things on your mind, ideas will appear. Sometimes, I can even use some of my scribble rants as parts of a future project so nothing is wasted. When you can unclutter your mind from the day's events, you'll be amazed at what you can achieve.

Since becoming an author, I have discovered that the ideas seem to come into my mind at the time when I am not in front of the laptop. Therefore, I use either the notes app on my phone or I always keep a notebook nearby to scribble down any idea that forms in any scenario. Sometimes this is key and other times, it's a lot of nonsense but ideas can literally spring from anything. Taking the dog for a walk and seeing two elderly women dancing in the field. What's their story? Watching someone in their car waiting at the traffic lights singing along to whatever song was playing on the radio at that time. What's his story? There are a wealth of opportunities around us everyday to explore someone else's life for our own literary gain. By no means do I tell everyone to stalk that person, check their mail, peruse their every social media post, but let them be your inspiration. If you were in their shoes, how would you react to scenarios? Why would you react that way? Is it right or wrong? And who has the right to judge?

This year, I am embarking on my first NaNoWriMo adventure to kickstart the fourth Blake Langford adventure, Wheel Of Deception. So far, I have a basic outline of how I would like the story to develop, some plot-points carried over from the third book to ensure continuity and a synopsis. Other than that, I am looking forward to seeing how my 2,000 words per day can develop this story throughout November. This could be inspired, it could be a complete disaster, but it will be fun to find out. I will share my progress and challenges along the way in future newsletters so please keep a look out for those.

Until next time, write on.

JR

Writing For Children

I never thought that I could write a children's story. After all, at almost 40 years old, my childhood was a lifetime ago and what was cool in the 80's and 90's is generally considered lame by today's standards so how do you bridge the gap to be cool with the kids once again?

Becoming a father for the first time in 2014, I soon realised the responsibility of being a parent far outweighed the majority of my daily concerns as my wife and I try our hardest to make the best life possible for this new life that we've brought into the world. This often leads to a return to childhood imagination and removing the mask that we display to the world in everyday life.

When was the last time you could let your inhibitions about the world around us go in favour of a cartoon, an animated film or even something as basic as nursery rhymes, counting numbers or adding significant meaning to letters of the alphabet. As adults, we become so consumed in our fast-paced social media heavy world that we forget the little things that mean so much. A scribbled drawing on a sheet of paper. The happy smile and dance when your child fits his/her blocks into the right shape sorter. What happened to that enthusiasm for the simple things in life? When did we lose that innocent abandonment of real world issues? Did we become bitter about the world around us not giving us what we expected or did we just get old?

I pondered these questions until my friend, Steve Boyce, produced his amazing idea for a local traffic cone named Cornelius and his friends who went out on adventures in this fantasy world with seemingly no limitations or expectations. Basing the storylines in the little village of Hythe where we both worked as postmen at the time seemed to give the characters a realistic setting for where their lives could unfold. My son who was 5 years old at the time, absolutely loved the concept and this in turn, led to my creative spark coming back after years of being locked away. I began adding bits and pieces to the original story and coming up with ideas that my son enjoyed. Soon, the

Cornelius Cone stories were being read in the local schools and that was when I suggested my ideas for future adventures to Steve.

To my surprise, Steve offered me the chance to pursue these extra storylines as a co-author to his series and from this, several new compilations of Cornelius Cone were written. From my own experience, the easiest way to discover what is going on in the minds of children today is to simply engage with them. Ask them what they like to read about. What their interests are and you would be surprised about what they tell you. Several of the Cornelius Cone adventures were based on stories that had been told to me by the children. In The Tale Of The Naughty School Teacher, for example, the children were meant to be playing rounders at school but the teacher only had three cones for the game. There were several cones outside the school gate where some roadworks were happening so the teacher used one of their cones so the game could go ahead. Likewise, The Tale Of The Talking Postbox was inspired by one of my son's parents who accidentally dropped their mobile phone into a postbox when they went to post some letters. The wealth of inspiration around us can inspire so many storylines, if only we stopped for a moment to recognise them.

Now in 2023, the Cornelius Cone adventures continue to inspire the local children and I have now begun a spin-off series called Bennie Barrier's Big City Adventures where Cornelius' friend leaves the quiet village and tries to make a new life in the big city. Whether I am writing for Cornelius or Bennie, the thought process is the same. What challenge can I place in front of them? How would my child react to this challenge? Is there any way that the main characters can interact with those around them to overcome the challenge? And what learnings can be taken away from this storyline? If you can answer these questions, you're well on your way to creating a world of escapism where you, and the children, can disappear into whenever you like and shut out the worries of the real world around us. That would be nice wouldn't it?

Until next time, write on!

JR

Can everyone stop ****** swearing!!

Swearing can often divide readers. Obviously, the age appropriateness of books can be a big factor in where your target audience is. The big question is how can you convey a realistic situation, albeit in dialogue or the reaction of something extraordinary, when swearing is so commonly used in day-to-day life?

It doesn't seem that long ago when any expletive in a novel would be frowned upon and often send readers away from the book they were reading. Fast-forward to 2023 and the majority of books have swearing included in the opening pages and then repeated frequently throughout the storyline.

In a world where we are more divided than ever before, how can you as an author tread the path of what is right and what is real? Some may say that we have become too cautious in our analysis of genders, race, sexuality and many types of discrimination and the end result is a "woke" mess that nobody fully understands or wants to engage with anymore.

With the increased spotlight on these issues, I tend to aim towards what I feel is the right balance of adventure and escapism whilst being aware of the circumstances and empathising with the characters in order to try and not fall foul of the "cancel culture" that exists today. So why is it such a thorny issue if the main character swears his way through the novel? Let's delve in a little deeper...

When you pick up a book in the library, download it to your e-reader or buy it from a bookshop, what are you looking for? We buy groceries because we need to eat. We buy juices and water because we need to drink. Why do you buy books? The overwhelming answer is one of escapism. With the advance of the internet and our 100mph lives that we now live, we are looking for that little moment of escape. To slow down. To live in someone else's life. At least for a little while, until the treadmill of life calls us back to reality again.

Social media is seen as the killer of the reader. How many people would be more likely to pick up their phone to look at Facebook, X/Twitter or Instagram than to pick up a book or even a magazine or newspaper? (Remember those) We have become so embroiled in wanting up-to-date information at our fingertips that we go online to search for one thing and end up down a rabbit hole of something else completely unrelated before realising that half an hour has passed and we need to get on with whatever it was we were doing before we were interrupted.

So do books still hold a place in today's world? Of course they do. We become so intoxicated with social media and the world around us that the need for escapism will always be needed. Even back centuries ago, our ancestors would gather around the campfire to hear folk tales from long ago to escape their current plight. So why is swearing in these circumstances a contentious issue?

Swearing tends to be a hallmark of the world we are looking to escape from. Like a jump-scare in a movie, it can shake you out of the scene and make you reconsider what you originally thought to be true. Although in today's world, swearing can be often used in every other sentence, especially in male-dominated areas, there is a fine line between what's real, what's right and what's accepted in escapism fiction.

Throughout the Blake Langford novels, I have tried to use swearing as sparingly as I can. Yet, without it, would a torture scene or a heated argument in a police station seem staged rather than realistic? I always consider if an F-bomb is needed or whether the point of the drama can be diverted elsewhere. Some will love the gritty realism, some will hate it. That's a matter of choice to the reader and who the author is aiming their book towards. There are many words that can cause offence and they are not necessarily classed as swear words per se, but I always remember what the great Billy Connolly once said; "A lot of people say that it's a lack of vocabulary that makes you swear. Rubbish. I know thousands of words but I still prefer f**k!" And on that note, I'll escape into my next novel.

Until next time, write on.

JR

Should Mental Health Issues Be Explored In Popular Fiction?

As with a lot of things in today's world, certain subjects can make people feel uncomfortable, knowing that a single innocuous comment can inevitably lead to the cancel culture taking aim at them. If the pandemic has taught us anything, it is the impact that mental health is having on us and why it shouldn't be ignored.

Male suicide especially is at an all time high and the older view of being told to "man up" and the stereotype that it is weak to show emotion still shows itself in male dominated environments today. This suppression of emotion slowly builds up a volcano of pressure that, if not released at some point, can lead to addiction, violence, depression, anxiety and in some cases, death. So why is mental health such a taboo subject in literature? If we want our stories, our characters and their scenarios to be realistic, surely we need to take into account their emotional needs as well as their physical desires and insecurities.

In a recent adventure that I wrote for the children's series that I co-author with my friend Steve Boyce, The New Adventures Of Cornelius Cone, there is a point in the story where Cornelius feels lost. Like there was no point in carrying on with the task and he removed himself from the job and went into the forest to sit alone with his thoughts. His friend, Bennie Barrier, noticed that he had left and followed him to where he was sitting alone looking out at the night sky. Instead of interrogating him, Bennie just sat with him and supported him in his moment of contemplation. Just being there whilst his friend worked through his own thoughts and troubles. The aim of this story was to show children that, on those days when you don't feel yourself, it's okay to take a moment to figure out what is going on in your mind without fear of intimidation, judgement or to even have all the answers to what is happening. It's okay just to feel human and to be yourself.

In my adult fiction, the main character, Blake Langford, is carrying the guilt from the first novel where he was unable to save the life of the woman he loved. Now, he has to adapt to a new life bringing up his son and adapting his professional life with his personal life. This juggling act can often lead to him acting irrationally, becoming frustrated and making snap decisions that he, at times, regrets later but this is his journey through the emotional rollercoaster of life that has been set out before him.

Even in our AI dominated world that we are living in, what connects us all is that human desire to be seen and be heard. Love, hate, anger, adoration, pleasure, pain, we feel it all so why hide it away? Do we think it's abnormal to have human emotions and challenges? When something annoys us, rather than bottling up the anger, is it unnatural to retaliate even if we regret our actions later? At the end of it, we're all human. We all do good and bad things. We achieve amazing feats and we also royally screw things up from time to time. That's life. To hide that from view due to the fear of being judged, cancelled or challenged can have devastating consequences.

Of course, I'm not condoning hate and malicious targeting of individuals who are different from each other. Everyone has a right to live the lives they choose. I believe that nobody wakes up in the morning with the sole intention to hurt somebody else. But having a more empathetic view of the people around us, the circumstances they have found themselves in, their journey up to this point and how they react to those things, can tell us a lot about who they really are. So, should mental health be discussed and explored in popular fiction? For me, if we ignore this, we are ignoring what it is to be human. Should I be cancelled for that viewpoint? I'll let you decide.

Until next time, write on.

JR

Is The 24/7 Online World Burning Us Out?

How much time do we spend on our phones, tablets, PC's and laptops per day? When was the last time you sat on a bus, train or as a passenger in a car and just looked out at the world as you passed by? More importantly, how many times have you sat at the dinner table with your family and rather than engage in conversation about their day, you felt the urge to update social media instead?

New technology that was meant to bring us all closer together has instead, made the world we live in, become more lonely than ever. In a doctor's waiting room or at a bus stop, everyone is staring at their phones. Nobody is willing to start a human conversation that doesn't involve screens anymore. Even phone calls are now reduced to short sharp text messages. We are losing the art of conversation and in this 24/7 information world, perhaps we're losing our minds too.

Over exaggerating? Let's dig a little deeper. Way back when we used to live in caves with our tribes, the average person would probably engage with up to 100 people in their lifetime from their local villages. They wouldn't have travelled far and there was no such thing as the internet or even newspapers back then. All the news came from hearsay. Somebody's aunt's second cousin heard that Dorothy from the end of the street has just given birth to twins. Whilst looking back on this as just being very restrictive, basic information, that has no bearing on today's world, even though technology has radically changed over the years, our brains have stayed the same.

We were never created to store millions of lines of information like today's modern systems are. We were never created to engage with thousands of people on a daily basis yet your social media post is viewed all over the world. Filters on our handpicked photos of the best moments of our lives make the world believe that we are all living our best lives. But the reality is, we're not. Those photos are the highlights amongst the ordinary, mundane life that the average person leads yet social media displays us as if we are famous celebrities looking for appreciation and acceptance. The problem is, a lot of the time, we get it too.

So, why is that a bad thing? In the modern day world, suicidal ideation and mental health issues have massively increased. Current statistics show that 1 in 8 of us will encounter some kind of mental health crisis in our lives. Why is that? Because everything is about comparison. Young impressionable men and women see these perfectly edited highlights clips online of how this person or that person is allegedly living their best lives. Then they look around and see the reality of their own lives forgetting that the video doesn't show the full story.

Life is for living and some have more privilege than others and that's okay, but we need to find what is right for us in our own circumstances to be the best version of ourselves in this world. Comparing yourself to a World Cup winning footballer when you've barely kicked a ball around a playground is always going to lead to disappointment and disillusionment. But being the best you can be, whether that is the best parent, the best cleaner, the best accountant, the best shopkeeper, the best author, whatever fulfils you in life, should be your aim and not the picture perfect life that is displayed on social media because, guess what, it's all a lie.

So, is our 24/7 online world burning us out? From the evidence we see on a daily basis, we seem to be in the pressure cooker already. It needs to be our own conscious decision whether we step out of it or not.

The reality is we are becoming a generation of online zombies. We're not robots and no matter how much artificial intelligence is interacting in our world, we will always be a human soul with our own needs, responsibilities, emotions, behaviours and quirks. We need to find a way to get back to being human again. When we find our connections, our hobbies, the things that bring us joy in this world and most of all, when we just sit down, take a breath, maybe drink a cup of coffee and ask the person next to you, how are you today?

You'll be surprised how good it feels to, in a way, step back in time and have a real conversation with another human being.

Until next time, write on.

JR

NaNoWriMo 2023 - When Life Gives You Lemons.... Write!

November is a magical time of the year, the build-up to Christmas, the fireworks lighting up the night sky and it's the month where writers like you and I knuckle down for a daily ritual to produce 50,000 words in 30 days.

For many years, I have planned to participate and for one reason or another, I have failed to stick to it but, despite life's best efforts to send in the distractions, 2023 will be the year for my NaNoWriMo experience. This would be the chance to write without restriction and to create a solid base for the fourth Blake Langford adventure, currently titled; Wheel Of Deception.

So, I set up a writing area in my spare room with the intention to write on November 1st when I hear a call from downstairs. When I go down to find out what's happening, I discover that someone has slashed one of our car tyres with a screwdriver. Despite the NaNo God's conspiring once again, I was able to change the tyre and finally settle in for day 1 later that evening, writing 1667 words. So far so good.

Then came day 2, November 2nd and storm Ciaran swept across the area. The grand plan of dropping my son at school and then settling down to write goes out of the window when an email from the school explains that it's too windy for the school to open. Somehow, I managed to control my scepticism as when I was younger, some wind and rain and even a few inches of snow was considered just a winter's day but again, the writing session was pushed back until the evening. Feeling a renewed focus on my NaNo project, I was now up to 3333 words after 2 days.

Day 3 comes along and we wake up to no running water after a landslip at the local water treatment centre led to supplies of water for the entire area being shut down until they could purify the water once again. Looking at my emails once again, the school has closed due to no running water and day 3's planned writing session has now turned into visiting local water stations to collect bottles of water for family and friends. Looking at this objectively, it gives me some great ideas and content for future projects but I'm beginning to think that this new NaNo project is jinxed. Thankfully, after a day of distractions, I finally managed to settle down and write, finishing day 3 with 5374 words so far.

Day 4 and 5 continued in the same vein. Collecting water, homeschooling and keeping the family entertained whilst my head is screaming at me to write. By the time everyone has gone to bed, the dreaded blank screen is in front of my eyes and do the words flow? No. Off to the scribble pad to declutter the brain and see if there is actually any gold at the end of this rainbow. Do us writers get a free pass for procrastination or is it just the role we have to endure? I'll let you decide.

So, why am I telling you all this? We all try to justify the reasons why we don't have time to write but the fact is, life will always throw a curveball into the mix of how we think our day will pan out. I once heard the quote; man plans, God laughs. Just because things don't always turn out the way we expect them to doesn't mean that this is necessarily a bad thing. Sometimes, the bad things that happen often set us up for good things further down the road. All we need to do is be aware of them and make the best of a bad situation.

I see the NaNoWriMo as an opportunity to create a new writing habit amongst a community of writers all aiming to either produce a finished piece of writing or at least, take significant steps towards a bigger project. Whether you write 20 words, 200 words, 2000 words or even 5000 words per day. Progress is progress, no matter how big or small. The important thing is that you do it.

For me, I finished writing my third Blake Langford novel several months ago and have been going through the editing process with the vain hope that the novel, In The Shadow Of My Life, will be ready to publish in time for Christmas. During this process I've become so familiar with the series again in 2023, it seemed like the obvious choice for NaNoWriMo to continue the series with the fourth Blake Langford novel. So, how to start? The fourth instalment follows on from the third book so, thankfully, a lot of the groundwork is already in place.

My Blake Langford adventures tend to range between 60,000-90,000 words so the 50,000 target for NaNoWriMo will be a significant step on the first draft of book 4. Whether any of what I have written so far will make it into the final book in 2024 remains to be seen.

So, after rambling when I should've been writing, my verdict is: don't give up! Even when life gives you lemons, you've got this!

My progress so far: Day 7 and 8375 words (17%) of my 50,000 words target. I'll see you again next week with the hope of a significant leap forward.

Until next time, write on.

JR

Who is Bennie Barrier?

Those of you who are familiar with the Children's books that I have written, alongside my friend Steve Boyce, as part of "The New Adventures Of Cornelius Cone" series will have often heard of Cornelius's friend, Bennie Barrier.

As Steve puts the finishing touches to his latest animated story, we wondered how we could add a new dimension to the series without alienating the current audience who have enjoyed the Cornelius Cone adventures so far. That was when my son asked, what if Cornelius Cone's friends had their own adventure too?

This sparked the idea for Bennie Barrier's Big City Adventures and a whole new spin-off series incorporating the same themes as the Cornelius Cone series. But how can you make a series that moves a minor character into the central role of the story without losing the interest of the reader?

We decided that we had to take Bennie Barrier out of Cornelius Cone's Maintenance Team on the edge of the New Forest, where he had his own friendships and was well known in the community, and move him into the city centre where his only connection to the world he left behind was his friend, Bruno Bus who occasionally gives us updates from Cornelius Cone's world. This allowed a new kind of adventure, taking advantage of all of the sights and sounds of Southampton City Centre and the busy nature of city life to completely immerse Bennie Barrier into his new world.

So, who is Bennie Barrier? Steve and I always wanted the stories to have a strong emphasis on recycling and being responsible members of the community. Therefore, Bennie's backstory is that he was originally made into crisp packets at a factory in Leicester and was recycled many times before he finally was created to be a roadside barrier. His introduction to the series was far from the loud, expressive characters that populated Cornelius Cone's world. When he arrives in "The Tale

Of The Missing Cone," he hides away in the corner of the yard, trying not to be noticed by anyone, just like the new kid in school.

Cornelius Cone then asks him to join in on an adventure to get Wet Floor back to the supermarket after he ended up at The Maintenance Yard by accident. Along the way, there are lessons in road safety, stranger danger and friendships that will hopefully strike a chord with many young children going through their primary school years today.

Most of all, we wanted Bennie Barrier to be real. That shy kid in the new class who feels awkward. A bit of an outcast. Maybe not quite as intelligent as those around him but his persistence and willingness to learn and try his best in all situations show that hard work and making the effort does pay off. This made him a strong and regular character in the Cornelius Cone series. So, who is Bennie Barrier?

Bennie is the one out of all of us who has a heart of gold but often gets overlooked and pushed out of situations. The one who is a thinker. Methodical and analytical in his approach to life. A loyal friend, enjoys a joke or two and often finds himself in situations that he is uncomfortable with but manages to make the best of the situation regardless of his knowledge. Most importantly, in a world of fantasy where children can escape to from time to time, Bennie Barrier experiences what it is like to be a child again. Innocent, inquisitive, fun, energetic and occasionally the odd one out as well as being the hero.

Bennie Barrier's Big City Adventures are available now from Amazon and all good bookshops worldwide.

Bennie Barrier's Big City Adventures - Volume 1: 12 Unmissable Adventures https://amzn.eu/d/cHgXAjo

Until next time, write on.

JR

In Case You Didn't Know, Self Publishing Is Hard Work But Don't Give Up!!!

We all had that dream didn't we? I'm going to pour my heart and soul out onto the paper, it's going to be beautifully bound in a paperback and hardback cover that's going to fly off the shelves, soon it'll be television deals and sipping champagne with famous authors, it's only a few clicks away and then..... no one buys it. You look at your sales figures on a daily basis and find 0. A big fat zero. Not even John down the road who said you were going to be the next superstar has parted with his cash to put a smile on your face. Family members who promised they would buy your book as soon as you released it are suddenly ignoring your calls. Social media posts that were previously getting 100 likes are now barely registering anything. Then the questions fill your mind as you look over the masterpiece that has dominated your every thought, your every waking moment of the past few years and you ask yourself, why?

Sound familiar? Believe me, you're not alone. In a world that is more technologically advanced than at any point in our history, we are left with two realities. Firstly, it is easier than ever to get your work published but secondly, it is harder than ever to have your work read by the public. Contradiction? Let's see...

In 2023, the amount of people reading for pleasure has dropped significantly. Today, we have more distractions than ever and multi-million pound/dollar companies are working tirelessly to capture any bit of your attention that they can grab. Why? Because eyes on their prized possession equals money. Money from sponsorship and advertisements mean that for companies to be successful, they have to gain and keep your attention. Before streaming services such as Netflix, Disney+ and Amazon Prime arrived on the scene, if you were enjoying a TV series, you had to wait until one of the TV channels decided to show the next episode, (usually a week apart) before you could discover what happened next. Now, thanks to these streaming giants, you can watch an entire series in one day if you choose to. That choice, whilst great for the consumer, has a knock on effect to other activities that we do in our daily lives. As a consequence, the average consumer would more often than not, decide to settle in and binge watch the latest drama on their streaming services before going to bed than settling down to read a couple of chapters of a favourite or new book.

So, how do self published authors compete for the attention of their readers without the financial clout of the streaming companies or the marketing power of an established publishing house? The answer, make something different. Something that will capture the limited attention span of your reader, make them put their phone down for a while and keep them coming back for more. Grab them with an enticing opening paragraph and never let them go until the satisfying conclusion. J.K. Rowling's Harry Potter series was rejected several times before it became a huge success. Likewise, a lot of the latest dramas and films are at least inspired by new authors and screenwriters creating something new. Something exciting. Something inspirational that will leap out and grab the limited attention that is available out there now. Only you can tell your story your way. Nobody else has lived your experiences or has your take on a situation. For example, if there was a group of four people who had an argument about something. You would have four different opinions of the same argument and all of them would be true. The individual perspective of every one of us dictates what we believe is true in our everyday world.

The main barrier new authors find is the lack of exposure, especially after you have published your first book. A lot of this is down to advertisement and most new authors struggle to find where to start. Granted, you won't sell many books if you include regular advertisements within the pages of your novel, but the exposure you can create through social media, attending book promotions at your local bookstores, libraries, schools, local markets and creating your own website can all help to bring attention to your work. The main question is; how can anyone buy your work if they don't know it exists? Scream and shout it from the rooftops, be proud of your work and engage everyone you meet into knowing about it. You never know who's listening.

Until next time, write on.

JR

NaNoWriMo 2023 - When Everything Is Blocking You From Writing.... Reset And Start Again

It's November 1st and you decide to tackle this year's NaNoWriMo with all of the enthusiasm, bravado and blind faith that no matter what life throws at you, you'll work it out along the way. By the way, does this post count towards my 50k? I guess not. Let's just put this down to procrastination then.

So, after oversharing my perils and pitfalls of week 1 of my NaNoWriMo journey for 2023 and my word count of 8375 words (17%) of the 50,000 words target, I was feeling hopeful that I could make significant steps forward in week 2 and guess what, it half worked. On day 14, I had achieved 14155 words (28%) of my 50,000 words target. Then week 3 turned out to be a disaster as a grand total of zero words were added to my total. This in turn, made me wonder, why we are so hard on ourselves when life gets in the way of our creativity.

After all, writing a novel tends to be a marathon rather than a sprint and this time of year tends to throw up many obstacles including preparing for Christmas. Therefore, even with the best will in the world, I am conceding defeat for the month of November but NaNoWriMo has still proven to me that I can commit to a way of writing and still make significant progress despite the challenges of daily life interfering with my writing schedule. The first draft of Wheel Of Deception, the fourth Blake Langford novel will still be written but realistically, the 50k words will now be completed throughout December and January too.

So rather than be disheartened by the failure to complete NaNoWriMo in November, I'm taking the opportunity to reset and start again. 2024 promises to be busy with several writing projects on the horizon and the community around NaNoWriMo has given me the enthusiasm to start venturing outside my current writing genres.

As well as adding to the word count, growing the awareness around the Blake Langford series, the Bennie Barrier's Big City Adventures series and the Cornelius Cone adventures is just as important as writing them. You can write the best stories in the world but if nobody knows they exist, you will find very few sales coming your way.

So, for those of you who are well on your way to your 50k, I salute you. Well done and I hope your endeavours will ultimately end up with the finished draft being published in the new year. For those of us who fell short of our lofty target, don't despair. Reset and start again. You're already a long way forward than where you were on November 1st. Remember, only you can write your story and your unique tale needs to be told.

Until next time, write on.

JR

Is An Author Website Worth The Hassle?

You've released your first book and are looking for marketing opportunities but which way do you turn? A good option is a cheap, easy to setup and maintain website. With the onset of AI, it has never been easier to get yourself online and the majority of businesses would not survive if they never had an online presence. So how can you make an author website work for you?

Social media is a massive opportunity to gain followers to your website and regular promotion on these platforms with interesting previews or taglines can often help with your sales too. When I launched my own website; www.CorneliusCone.co.uk[1] on the GoDaddy platform in 2020, I was instantly engaging with people who were interested in the Cornelius Cone series and they found value in the extra blogs, updates and little snippets from the series that I uploaded regularly.

The key to maintaining your website and your audience is consistency. You need to make a conscious effort to consistently update the website to keep people engaged. Why do people love scrolling through social media? Because there is a new feed of information constantly recurring and your website should be no different.

When I launched the Cornelius Cone website, it was primarily for the co-author series that I was working on with my friend, Steve Boyce. However, over time, I've also been able to offer some promotional space to other writers as well as include my own writing journey on there too. Even though the domain has remained the same, the website now also includes my other projects, Bennie Barrier's Big City Adventures and The Blake Langford Adventures too.

The most important thing is to make the website work for you. The options are endless. If you have merchandise, you can create an online shop, advertise local book signing events or promote a preorder for your next book. Steve and I currently have three preorders that will

---

1. http://www.corneliuscone.co.uk

land in the coming months; Cornelius Cone And The Earth's Crust, Bennie Barrier's Big City Adventures - Volume 1 & In The Shadow Of My Life - The Third Blake Langford Adventure. All of these are promoted through the website as well as social media and it does make a significant contribution to the end result.

So, is an author website worth the hassle? Like our community here on Substack, the website is what you make of it. If you just upload your original content and leave it there, it is likely to grow stagnant and nobody will give it attention. But, like when you plant seeds, if you water it regularly, (keep it updated) and let it have sunlight, (exposure to the world via social media and word of mouth) then it will bloom into a beautiful flower.

Until next time, write on.

JR

How To Adapt Real Life Into Your Writing

Have you ever thought of using real life conversations and incidents in your writing but worried in case someone recognised themselves in your work?

The reality is, whether we realise it or not, we are picking up subtle cues from the people around us, those we watch on TV as well as our friends and family. If you sit in a coffee shop and look around, you have the business man in the suit, the mum who's trying to keep her child entertained, the young teenage couple on what was probably one of their first dates together and the two elderly ladies in the corner who have seen it all before. Just in those four examples are a multitude of storylines. What brought them to that coffee shop at that moment in time? What are their family lives? Do they work? If so, where and what do they do? Are they escaping a toxic environment at home or at work? Are they avoiding someone or waiting for a loved one to arrive? The possibilities are endless.

So, how can you encapsulate all of this into your stories without blatantly singling out someone who will recognise themselves in your work? Some people will happily be involved and will love being part of your project. Others will hate it.

When I used to work as a postman, we had two people in our office who really enjoyed the Cornelius Cone series that I was writing with my co-author, Steve Boyce. When we asked if we could include them in the stories, they were happy to be part of it. Soon after, Postman Pete and Grandad Cone were created. Postman Pete with his bad jokes and clumsiness as well as being part of a local band. Grandad Cone with his pretending to be deaf and mishearing what people are saying as well as his catchphrase, "What's happening then?" The same catchphrase that our work colleague used to always say when he entered the office.

Basing your characters on real life examples can often help make them feel real to the readers of your work. After all, they are real people to you in real life so you can use all of their traits, characteristics and mannerisms to add a realistic feel to your storyline. There is obviously a catch to all of this though. What if your opinion of somebody is less favourable and paints them in a bad light?

In Bennie Barrier's Big City Adventures, Jumpstart Jo, the city jumplead is identified as a chatterbox who constantly complains about everything. Rather than base her on a single character, I have used the traits of several characters to make this hyperactive individual come to life. Unfortunately, if someone identifies themselves with these traits, this can obviously have a bad knock on effect and you could potentially land yourself in hot water if people, places and scenarios are identified as being the obvious traits of someone you know. The best way that I can find around this is to make your characters have multiple quirks and mannerisms so that there is some wiggle room for creative licence to get you out of any potential trouble.

Some of the ways to use the tools that are around you is to sometimes manipulate the situations to serve a purpose without victimising anyone. For example, two people that I know, will happily belch and fart in public with no shame whatsoever. Rather than encapsulate that in a character that they would recognise, Steve and I based the mannerisms of Bertie Bin from those people but also gave Bertie a childish and jokey characteristic to dilute the crudeness and make the character more fun.

On a more serious character trait, my first Blake Langford adventure; Where No One Stands Alone, features Blake's struggle as he comes to terms with the loss of the love of his life. I had recently come out of a long term relationship before writing this novel and looking back now, a lot of Blake's emotional turmoil in that storyline was partly taken from my own situation at that time. With the wealth of subject matter surrounding us, sometimes, we can also find fascinating details if we just learn to look at our own lives objectively too.

So, is it worth using real life scenarios and people in your writing? You decide, but make sure that those you do engage with are happy with your interpretation of their character and for your own peace of mind, piece together your characters with small snippets of several people so if anyone is offended or recognises themselves, you have the creative excuses ready.

Until next time, write on!

JR

In The Shadow Of My Life - The Third Blake Langford Novel - Exclusive Preview

As a thank you to everyone who takes the time to read my Substack each week, I would like to share the Prologue and first chapter of the latest Blake Langford adventure with you. If you've read any of the Blake Langford adventures previously, you will notice that this book follows on directly from the second adventure; Underneath The Covers.

The synopsis of In The Shadow Of My Life is;

When a London Underground Train makes an unscheduled stop at a disused station, Blake Langford realises that something is not quite right.

As he follows the abandoned staircase up into a rundown building above the station, he discovers the body of a young girl.

As Blake pursues the case, London's cruel streets provide little explanation of who the girl was or how she was killed until a surprise confession from his sister changes the case completely.

When blood runs thicker than water, Blake is left with two women wanting answers and a brother in need of an alibi, but who can he trust?

Intrigued so far? If so then enjoy this exclusive preview of the novel before it's publication and I'd love to hear your thoughts on it so far.

Prologue

"So you'll be there?," Jenny asked.

"On my way, just make sure Paula doesn't suspect anything," came the reply as the phone call ended.

Jenny Langford took a deep breath before heading into the lounge. It was a cold Friday evening in January and snowflakes were falling softly outside 124 Alfredson Road in Kensington, the family home of Blake Langford's mother, Emily Langford. Blake's sister, Jenny and Paula, his partner, were there whilst Emily played games with her grandson, Michael. After returning from his previous assignment in Edinburgh, Blake had some business to attend to in the city before returning to the family home.

Michael was sitting at the dining table painting a sword and shield cut out of a cardboard box alongside his grandmother. Emily was glad to have the family back home again after they had been caught up in Blake's recent investigation involving a corrupt Scottish Police Detective.

"Are you two okay whilst Paula and I nip out for a bit?" Jenny asked.

"Of course," Emily replied as she helped Michael wash off one of the paint brushes.

"Only if you bring some donuts back!" Michael replied.

"Deal!" Jenny laughed before leading Paula out towards the hall.

"Where are we going? I thought Blake wanted us to stay here until he gets back," Paula asked as they slipped on their coats.

"Come on Paula, we need to relax and have a bit of fun. I know this really nice bar near Waterloo Station."

Paula looked back at Michael happily painting at the dining table.

"He'll be fine. Mum will look after him," Jenny continued before opening the front door.

"Okay, one drink," Paula sighed before heading out of the door.

They wandered down towards the London Underground station and took the Circle Line towards Embankment before emerging near Westminster on the opposite side of the River Thames from Waterloo Station. The London Eye lit up the night sky and reflected off of the river as they crossed Westminster Bridge.

"I forgot how magical the city could be at night time," Paula said as they looked across the river.

"Do you regret moving away?" Jenny asked.

"Sometimes. It's hard to build any friendships when you're isolated in the countryside. My judgement of character is obviously floored too as proven by Simone."

Simone Shaubena had been involved in Blake's recent investigation which led to Paula, Jenny and Michael being held captive in the dungeons of Tallon Castle.

"That was an exceptional circumstance. Blake has a lot of enemies and they used his family ties to get to him."

"And that's just it. I'm constantly having to look over my shoulder. Constantly having to vet everyone I come into contact with in case there's an ulterior motive to their interest in me."

"Blake will never let anything happen to you or Michael."

"I know."

"I feel there's a "but" there."

"When Andy was taken away, I vowed that I would never let a man dictate my life again. My writing and my art were my escape from that world. I always wanted to be the hero of the story. Live happily ever after. I often would come out at night and look at the lights and people rushing from place to place in the city. I wondered what their lives would be like. Their worries, their ambitions, their relationships, I craved to be out of my bubble and to see the world."

"Then Rachael changed that."

"I love my sister but I hated what she did to Blake. He's a good man and he loved her with all of his heart. Mum and dad would never agree to their relationship. Thought Blake's job was too dangerous and she was too young for him to be involved with."

"They didn't trust him?"

"We all made mistakes when we were younger."

"I know what it's like to have a father that disapproves of everything you do," Jenny admitted. "Steven moved away to escape Dad's judgement. Blake was always out on missions with Special Branch and I was left to be the dutiful daughter tending to our parents' needs."

"Your Mum seems to have things under control now."

"When Dad became ill, things were hard for her. She turned to alcohol to block things out but she worked her way through it and rebuilt her life after he died."

"Did you ever want a relationship or your own little family?" Paula asked.

"I'm too close to forty for all of that now."

"That's not a no."

"There was this one guy, Tom."

"What happened?"

"He was in the forces and was killed in Iraq."

"I'm sorry, I didn't..."

"It's okay. We were only together for six months but in that time I felt like I'd never felt in my life before. I can't even describe the feeling."

"It's just special."

"Yes, special," Jenny smiled as she began leading them along the path towards the London Eye. "Is that how Blake makes you feel?"

"That's deep."

"It's honest."

"We have history..."

"I know."

"For so long I've been in Rachael's shadow. Her disappearance and reappearance in America. Her relationship, if you could call it that with

James Turner. She always was adamant that her and Blake would be together in the end."

"You gave them both that opportunity when you asked Blake to go to Miami and save her."

"And when he couldn't, he was destroyed."

"Even the roughest of diamonds can still shine."

"Meaning?"

"If you were on your deathbed, would you rather have regrets for not doing something or the knowledge that even if it didn't work out, you gave it your best shot."

Paula looked up at the London Eye.

"Rachael has gone Paula. No matter what we do or the circumstances we find ourselves in, we can't change that. Michael looks upon you as the mother figure in his life now. Blake is his father. You have the chance to create something beautiful here," Jenny continued.

At that moment, Paula looked at the metal platform in front of The London Eye and saw Blake dressed in a suit holding a bouquet of roses. He beckoned for her to join him. Paula turned to Jenny who gently pushed her forwards. A crowd of people had gathered nearby as Paula walked up the steps to join Blake on the platform. He led Paula onto one of the glass capsules and the operator closed the door before they began to slowly rise up into the night sky.

"I'm sorry Jenny had to lead you astray," Blake smiled as he handed the flowers to Paula.

"You certainly are full of surprises," Paula smiled.

"I remember one time when I was working and I saw you sat on the opposite side of this river looking up at the eye and the lights. It's amazing to think that we're so busy in our everyday lives that we forget to notice the beauty of who and what is around us."

"London lights used to be my escape from reality. My hope for a better life..."

"I've made many mistakes over the years. I've gone head first into situations that I shouldn't have. I've been reckless and stubborn. I guess I get that from my parents. In my job, a split-second decision often is the difference between life and death. I've been running for too long. Running away from things that scare me. Things that force me into making rash decisions. I'm not going to run away anymore..."

"What do you mean?"

"I mean that I want to write a new chapter, build a new future, with you..."

Blake placed his hand inside his pocket and pulled out a navy blue box. He knelt down on one knee and opened the box to reveal a sapphire and diamond ring.

"Paula Evans, will you marry me?"

Tears stung her eyes as she looked at the ring and then at Blake.

"Yes, of course, yes!"

Blake stood up and wrapped his arms around her. Paula held him close for what felt like an eternity. She had found the love and security that she had craved for so long. When they parted, Blake slipped the ring on her finger.

"Why now?"

"I had a lot of time to think when we were in Scotland. When I thought I was going to lose you both again, it ripped me apart. I've made so many mistakes Paula and now I need to start making choices that I've been too afraid to make in the past. That's starting with commitment, to you and to Michael. No matter what, you two are my life now."

As the glass capsule arrived back at the platform and both Paula and Blake stepped out, a small group of people applauded as they walked down the exit ramp hand in hand.

Jenny rushed over and hugged them both. "Congratulations to you both! Sorry for misleading you."

"I'll forgive you just this once," Paula teased. "So what now?"

"Well I know a place in Leicester Square that we can go to," Blake suggested.

"I'll head back, I don't want to be a third wheel..." Jenny began.

"No, no, come with us, we're family now," Paula insisted.

They wandered over towards Waterloo Station together before heading down the escalators towards the tube. The train whooshed into the station and they climbed aboard before the doors closed and they were on their way again. Three other passengers glanced in their direction as they sat near one of the doors. They passed through Embankment and Charing Cross underground stations before heading off towards Leicester Square. As the train left Charing Cross station, they heard a loud screeching metal against metal sound before the train came to an abrupt stop.

"What's going on?" Paula asked.

"I don't know but I'm sure we're better off out than in," Blake replied as he walked over towards the door and used the emergency exit release to open the door.

"Hey man! What are you doin'?" one of the passengers called out. "That's suicide stepping out there!"

"Blake! What are you doing?" Jenny gasped.

"It's an old disused station. There's no point waiting an hour for the rescue team to come down here. Come on!"

Blake jumped down from the train before helping Paula and Jenny down.

"Are you sure this is safe?" Paula asked.

Blake held his phone torch out in front of him and headed towards the back of the platform. "This is the old freight line that used to be in service during the war. Come on, this way!"

"This is not the romantic evening I had planned for you two," Jenny sighed.

Blake found the staircase and began climbing up. "This will get your steps in for the day."

"Seriously?" Jenny complained.

"It's only about two hundred steps to the top," Blake laughed.

The metal stairs spiralled round and round from the depths of the underground network all the way back up to the streets of London above them. After a couple of stops and some swearing, Jenny and Paula finally caught up with Blake at the top of the stairs.

"Don't... ever... make... me... do... that... again!" Jenny snapped.

"Haven't you had enough of running around underground lately?" Paula asked.

"I think we've got bigger problems than a huge staircase," Blake replied.

As Blake shined the light from his torch at the far corner of the room, Jenny and Paula both screamed. Staring back at them was the dead body of a young girl.

Chapter One

The Brother And The Dead

Two Weeks Later

"Fractured skull, neck broken, signs of sexual assault although we're still running tests," Sergeant Shaun Bryant confirmed.

"Do we know who she is?" Joe Knight asked.

"We found her student card in her purse. Everything else was taken."

"Convenient."

"Quite."

"This is the second one we've found. Have they informed the next of kin?"

"Eric Gordon's arranging that once the ID has been confirmed. We're looking for one seriously messed up son-of-a-bitch here."

Joe sighed. "What type of person would rape and kill a student and then, rather than hide or bury the body, they throw it off of a bridge on to one of the busiest roads in the south?"

"To send a message?"

"To whom?"

"That's what we need to work out."

"This can't leak out."

"With all due respect, Sir, the media are all over it. We need to give them something."

"They have their story. A young girl commits suicide on the A34. That's all they need to know."

"And what about the trafficking of foreign students?"

"No comment."

"The CIA are starting to get itchy feet already. It's only a matter of time before they come over and investigate for themselves."

"That's where you come in," Joe snapped, walking over to his desk, pulling a blue folder out of a drawer and handing it over to Sergeant Bryant. "That is the file of mugshots for all the missing students across the country. Now whoever is behind this has given us one. He's obviously one for melodrama. We need to find the others before he pulls another stunt like this. Speak to their families again. Gain as much knowledge as possible on them whilst Special Branch work on taking this group down."

"And what makes you think they'll say anything to me that's not already on record?"

"Because I have an eighteen year old American girl in the morgue who needs justice. Gordon's pulling the strings to get our men in place. Until we get a formal ID on this girl, it remains classified. Am I understood?"

Bryant nodded.

"Good. I need those statements yesterday. If we can find any kind of pattern, we might be able to find out where they're going to strike next."

Sergeant Shaun Bryant left the room as Joe Knight sat back in his chair, feeling the weight of the case heavy on his shoulders. He couldn't help but think about the dead girl, who was just a year younger than his own daughter. He shook his head to clear the thought and focused on the task at hand.

He flicked through a scattering of paperwork before filing it into the bin. He pulled his phone out of his pocket and scanned through his contacts list. He stopped at Langford 27942. He jotted the phone number down onto a notepad before locking his phone and returning it to his pocket. A photo of his wife, Patricia and his daughter, Carla, stared back at him from beside his laptop screen.

"It's time," he said before picking up his suit jacket from the back of his chair and walking out of the door.

***

The early spring sunshine sparkled on the morning dew that clung to the grass of the old cemetery on the edge of The New Forest. Blake knelt beside a newly erected headstone and placed some fresh daffodils into its rose bowl. As he stood once again, he took in a deep breath and sighed. The gold writing inscribed into the marble stone had a sense of finality about it. For the past few months, he tried to dismiss the reality that Rachael was gone. That it was some kind of bad dream that he just needed to wake up from. Seeing her name on the stone however, cut him deep once more.

"I hope you understand," Blake said softly, his hand brushing against the top of the gravestone as he walked by before heading back towards his car.

As he arrived at the cemetery gates, Blake noticed a man standing by his silver Ford Mondeo wearing a dark suit, white shirt, black tie and perfectly polished black shoes.

"I'm sorry for your loss Blake," the man said as Blake approached his car.

"Joe Knight, they finally let you out from behind a desk?"

"Briefly, you caused quite a shitstorm up north."

"If they wanted Ramon's soul they should have sent a priest. Unfortunately too much was left in the hands of amateurs. So what brings you down here?"

"We need to establish protection for yourself and your family."

"Frank Jackson, the agent that Gordon sent, is already here. My family are fine. We live in a quiet little village by the sea," Blake replied.

"And yet your son and partner have almost become collateral damage in your previous two assignments."

Blake sighed. "I take it this isn't a social call Knight so what is it?"

"We need you in London. Something big's going down."

"Gordon has my number."

"And he'd have used it if it was his case."

"I'm not for hire," Blake replied as he opened the driver's door.

"Eliza Lewis."

"What about her?"

"Old friend?"

"Irrelevant."

"Scottish student murdered ten years ago and then mysteriously turns up at a local newspaper as a journalist uncovering a major news story. I understand she got under your skin too..."

"Get to the point."

"Twelve students have disappeared in the past six months. You stumbled upon one in that old underground station and we found one of them tossed from a motorway bridge on the A34 overnight."

"How has this been kept out of the media? Twelve students, surely they've been missed by families and friends."

"You'd think so but so far we've come up with nothing. The only thing found on her was a student card, Victoria Louise Dawson, eighteen years old from Shreveport, Louisiana, attending Kings Cross University, London."

"Very convenient, has the university been contacted for a formal ID?"

"A formal ID isn't possible considering how she was found but every avenue is being explored."

Blake shook his head. "I'm not your guy Joe. My team..."

"I know all about Mo and Peter."

"I can't attack a case like this alone. I need specialist people I can rely on and bounce ideas off of. People who I can trust to have my back when the shit hits the fan."

"Then we'll form a new team. Get your stuff and meet me in the blue room tomorrow morning," Joe replied, handing Blake his card before wandering over towards his own car.

Blake looked at the card. The blue room was Special Branch's undercover offices in Vauxhall, London. He watched the dust cloud rise and fall on the gravel track as Joe Knight drove away before he climbed into his car and headed back to Aunt Mary's holiday home at Lepe Beach. Blake had inherited the house after her death and he wanted it to become the family home for his new life with Paula and Michael. As he parked his car on the driveway, he saw Paula standing in the doorway.

"Where's Frank?" Blake asked as he approached the front door.

"On the beach kicking a football around with Michael," Paula sighed. "You're going back in again aren't you?"

"You spoke to Knight?"

"He asked where you were. Frank said he used to work with you."

"I'm sorry."

"For what?"

"Not being here. I should be kicking a ball around with Michael. You shouldn't need a bodyguard. How are we meant to have a normal family life when..."

"We don't have a normal family life. It's the job Blake. I knew what I was signing up for. When shit happens, you have to deal with it."

Blake leant against the wooden post at the entrance to the porch.

"Why don't we come with you?" Paula asked.

"To London?"

"Yeh, the change will probably do us all some good. We can see a few friends. Michael wants to see Arsenal play and you won't have to worry about us being isolated down here."

Blake moved forward and Paula leant into his chest wrapping her arms around his waist. Her long blonde hair brushed across his face in the breeze as he held her close. His mind was transported back a couple of weeks to that cold January night when they were alone on the London Eye together. After overcoming his doubts and fears, he finally gathered up the courage to ask Paula to marry him. Since that day, both of them had felt a closeness that they never had experienced before. A renewed focus that no matter what life was going to throw at them, somehow they would make it through.

"Okay," he said as they headed inside.

***

Later that night, a loud knocking on the front door of 124 Alfredson Road woke Emily Langford out of a deep sleep. She looked at the clock on her bedside table before staggering towards the bedroom door. She slipped on her dressing gown and wandered downstairs towards the front door.

"Who is it?" she called out as she lifted the key from the hook in the hallway.

"Mum, it's me!"

"Steven? For goodness sake, it's three a.m."

"I know, I'm sorry. I locked myself out and didn't have anywhere else to go."

Emily opened the front door and gasped when she noticed her youngest son standing there with blood all over his hands and t-shirt. "What on Earth has happened?"

"Nothing, there was a fight at Renda's Bar that got a bit out of hand," Steven replied as he entered the house. "I just need to get cleaned up. Is it ok to sleep here tonight?"

"Yes, of course. I think Blake left a couple of shirts in the spare room that should fit you. I'll make some tea."

Steven disappeared upstairs whilst Emily wandered into the kitchen to fill up the kettle and prepare their drinks. When he returned, he noticed his mum was sitting at the kitchen table staring outside at the night sky.

"Mum? Are you okay?"

"Oh Steven, I never heard you come in. Would you like some tea? she asked.

"Yes, it's okay, I'll make it..." Steven replied as Emily began to stand up from the chair before losing her balance and falling back into the chair.

Steven quickly moved to stop the chair from overbalancing and steadied her once again.

"Are you sure you're okay? I'm sorry if I woke you from a deep sleep."

"I'm okay, it's just a headache John. You go back to bed. I'll be fine."

Steven pulled his phone out of his pocket and scrolled down to his sister Jenny's number. It rang several times before going into her answerphone.

"Jen, it's Steven. I think mum's ill, call me as soon as you get this!" Steven said before cutting off the call.

Emily sat in the chair looking out at the night sky as he prepared two cups of tea before sitting beside her at the kitchen table.

"Oh, hello Steven, I didn't hear you come home. Make sure Jenny lets Milo out in the morning before she goes to work," she said before reaching for her cup of tea.

Steven held the cup to assist her as she took a sip of the tea.

"I'm not incapable of drinking a drink!" she snapped.

Steven moved his hands away slowly, not taking his eyes off of his mum's face. He noticed the right side of her face was starting to droop. He was about to speak when Emily dropped her cup spilling the hot tea across the table.

"Oh now look at what you've made me do!" Emily snapped as she tried to stand up.

"It's ok mum, wait there. I will sort it out!" Steven replied as he rushed over to pick up a cloth to clean up the spillage.

As he began cleaning up the spillage, his phone rang. He answered it without looking at the caller ID.

"You'd better not be drunk!" Jenny snapped.

"Jen, I think Mum's having a stroke, get an ambulance to the house quick!"

In The Shadow Of My Life will be released in December 2023 and will be available from Amazon and most bookstores worldwide.

Until next time, write on.

JR

Will AI Lead To The End Of My Life As An Author?

There has been a lot of talk lately regarding the publication of AI books that are flooding the market and making it even more difficult for first time authors to break through and get themselves noticed. Whilst the progress that has been made in the past few years has been immense, the general opinion of AI work has been lukewarm at best. Many stories that AI has published have been repetitive, lacking any emotional depth and have left a lot of readers underwhelmed. So, can or more importantly should AI be used to help to assist authors as they create their masterpiece?

The reality of today's world means that we interact with artificial intelligence on a daily basis. The google search on your phone, your satnav, your Alexa, the self service checkout at the supermarket, various types of AI are all around us. Recent studies have shown that AI bots are now learning from various writing programmes used by authors and are in some ways, plagiarising their work. Does this mean that your copyright is worthless?

I can see the advantages of using AI programs such as Grammarly for punctuation and general grammatical improvements on the author's manuscript after the first draft has been written. However, when it comes to generating ideas, writing whole sentences, paragraphs or chapters, we get into the minefield of what is your own work and what is the work of AI?

For me, the personal touch from an author using their own style, their own voice for their characters and giving them a fully rounded personality and believability is something that, I personally believe, AI cannot replicate. Being a huge fan of Lee Child's Jack Reacher series and Ian Fleming's original James Bond series, I believe that those authors had the fully rounded character in their mind when making decisions on the scenarios that their protagonists would find themselves in. Having that human touch and a realistic understanding of how each of us will likely react in any given scenario is what puts the human authors ahead of their AI equivalents.

Yes, AI will have trillions of lines of data. It will have a super intelligence of the like we have never seen before but bigger and bolder isn't always better. When the ebook was launched, it was feared that it would be the end of the line for paperback and hardback books. Yet, most bookstores are now more popular than ever. When I go away on holiday, having my Kindle with me so I can access a whole library of content is both convenient and saves a lot of space and weight in the suitcase. Yet, opening a brand new book by my favourite author, the feel of the spine, the smell of the pages, the staying awake to read just a couple more pages to finish the chapter before going to sleep, that's the real world experience and as far as I'm concerned, that is one area that AI will never reach.

Until next time, write on.

JR

It's All Been Done Before, There's Nothing New To Write About. Or Is There?

As writers, we can often become demoralised when the dreaded writer's block hits. When the words don't seem to flow. When your brain just can't seem to formulate any ideas and you're left wondering if there is anything new or original left to write about.

After all, storytelling has been a staple of human life since the dawn of humanity when people would gather around the campfire and share their stories and experiences with the rest of the group. So, is there anything new to write about and what makes your take on a tale unique?

The answer lies within you. A group of four people could have an argument about something and when the story is retold to people who were not there, it will have four different tales of the same argument. How? I hear you ask. Because we all interpret things differently. The instigator of the argument will always think that he/she/they are right and the person with the opposing viewpoint will often think that they are right and the instigator is wrong. Whichever way the argument goes, all four people will have different biases of the same argument and therefore, their viewpoint will be skewed one way or another.

The same can be said of storytelling. We may well have exhausted the majority of the stories in today's world. The traditional love story. The police procedural. The child horror. The Sci-fi adventure. But none of them have been told by you with your unique characters, quirks, amusing tales, outrageous comeuppances or dialogue. Only you can write your story from your perspective.

In the James Bond film Skyfall, James Bond blows up his old family home after setting traps for the villains to walk into. A lot of people called this film James Bond meets Home Alone after the Christmas movie starring Macaulay Culkin. Skyfall is a completely different movie to the family friendly Home Alone, however, comparisons were drawn due to the similar content. But when does similarity roll into plagiarism?

Plagiarism is generally seen as the use of another person's work, words or ideas without their permission or attribution however, as shown in the Skyfall example, ideas used in other films/books etc can be recycled providing you can give the idea your own twist with enough differences to make it unique. After all, how many stories involve the character traits of well known characters that we know in everyday life. The ideas have to come from somewhere and no matter how much we try to create our own unique ideas, authors will be subconsciously influenced by the books they read and the media they consume.

So when the writing block hits and you need to find a spark of inspiration, don't despair. As a writer, I tend to let my characters go and do whatever they want and then write down what I see. For example, if I'm sitting in a coffee shop, I can observe character 1 is scrolling on their phone, character 2 is reading the newspaper, character 3 looks fed up and just wants to be anywhere else but here and the waitress is rushing around in a vain attempt to keep everyone happy but is she really in the zone or just counting down the hours until she leaves?

There is inspiration everywhere. If you can't go out and observe people, turn on your TV. What's the story behind the newsreader's blank expression as they read the headlines? How would you react if you were in the jungle on that nature programme and came face to face with a leopard dissecting its prey? Does the quiz host secretly think that the contestant has no chance of winning the top prize? If so, how do they feel about that?

The statement that there are no new ideas to write about may, in part, be true. The initial idea may be the same but you have a unique viewpoint on this idea, don't waste your time thinking it's all been done before, think, what if I did things differently? What if person X reacted this way? What thoughts and feelings are they hiding within? That's where the magic happens.

Until next time, write on.
JR

Can The Local History Give You A New Inspiration For Your Novel?

I have discovered on my writing journey that inspiration is all around us. Whether it be a selection of people sitting in a coffee shop and you examine what their life story could be, to the man who regularly visits the supermarket every morning for his basket of groceries, or the faces you see on the early morning bus ride to work. Everyone and everything has a story behind it. I found inspiration for a section of my new Blake Langford novel by walking through a cemetery in The New Forest and wondering, how would Blake react to an arm hanging out of one of the graves? Morbid I know but it gave me a hook for the fourth book.

The same kind of idea sprung up when we visited London a few years ago and the Underground Train stopped for a couple of minutes between stations before continuing on to its destination. Again, I thought how would Blake react? Would he get out of the train? What would he find down here? That became the synopsis of In The Shadow Of My Life, the third Blake Langford novel.

But what role does local history play in our creation of fiction novels? The part I enjoy about writing fiction is the fact that you can use creative licence to enhance the storyline and make it more interesting, confrontational, even more outlandish than the everyday world we see around us. However, if you are setting your work in the past, you need to remain true to the people, the languages, the surroundings and the way of life that our ancestors lived. After all, you wouldn't expect the characters on programmes such as "Downton Abbey" to be using mobile phones or calling an Uber to take them to different places would you?

In today's world of having the internet at our fingertips, any inaccuracies in your historical piece will stick out like a sore thumb. Likewise, our thirst for knowledge also means that we are more drawn into historical storytelling than ever before. Knowing where you are going is just as important as knowing where you are from. My next Blake Langford novel will be set in 1948 and 2008 so research is key. How did people talk in 1948? Where did the children play? What games would they play? How different were people's lives in post-war Britain?

As the years pass and the older generations begin to pass away, a wealth of history dies with them. Sometimes, those stories that grandparents often recite about their younger years can contain gold mines of ideas and information. Likewise, in my local area, we have the oldest working Pier and train that is over 100 years old. Using little pieces of history like this can give your writing authenticity as people today can actually visit and see what you are describing in your novel.

So, can local history give you some new inspiration for your novel? The stories are there if you make the effort to dig deep enough into your research and confirm that your account matches that of the time you set your work in. Don't try to be the smartest person in the room and fall short, absorb information like a sponge and learn from those who were there at the time and your historical fiction will hit the right tones.

Until next time, write on.

JR

Why Is Research So Important When Writing Your Novel?

The old adage of writing about what you know is well known but sometimes, our own knowledge can become a limiting factor when writing fiction. Sometimes, you need to allow your imagination to run away with itself, especially on the first draft. Who knows, that crazy idea that you thought was ridiculous may find a plausible way into your final story.

A lot of fiction writing I find tends to be autobiographical. What I mean by that is, subconsciously or otherwise, you will tend to take your own thoughts, feelings and emotions into account when writing your character's plight. How would you react if a terrorist suddenly corners you? How would you react if a family member died? How would you react on the birth of your first child or their first day at school or if they went missing? All of your thoughts, feelings and reactions will bleed into the characters that you are writing. Whether that be from personal experience of those scenarios, whether you've witnessed a friend or relative in that situation or it can even be from watching a similar drama unfold on TV. Everything around us influences how we write, how we build our characters up and how we attempt to make them human to us, to the reader, as if we could walk down the street, meet them for the first time yet know everything about them.

So why is research so important if we can just base our characters on ourselves? When writing your novel, characters tend to move the story forwards but the locations, the mannerisms, descriptions of circumstances which the main protagonist finds themselves in are equally important to making your reader believe they are there. A story set in Victorian times will have a vastly different feel to one that is written in the present day.

Research is key to giving your storyline a believable timeline but a lot of authors tend to delve in too deeply with their research as it is easier to glean facts, figures and information from the internet rather than recycling that knowledge in the form of a novel. A lot of authors fall into the trap of creating a list of ten or more facts from their research and they then use this list as a tick-box exercise to make themselves look intelligent. Whilst the facts and figures are needed for a non-fiction book, a work of fiction is just that, fiction. You have researched the context for your book, for example 1980's crime drama, you have your main characters, some idea of the scenario they are getting themselves into and what the end result will be. Having a rigid ten item checklist is going to stifle creativity here. You need your characters to get from point A to point B but it doesn't need to be a rigid format. Experiment a little. On your first draft, go for the most extraordinary, crazy, outlandish thing you can think of. This can always be edited and pulled back in the second or third drafts. Use your research as a guideline to help you get your story from start, to middle and then to a satisfactory conclusion at the end but don't let it turn into a paint-by-numbers exercise, it will bore you and in turn, it will bore your readers.

So, is research really important when writing your novel? I'd give the answer of partly yes, partly no. Realism shouldn't get in the way of your creativity and imagination but likewise creativity and imagination shouldn't lead you to describing the inner workings of social media to Henry VIII. Your research is your all you can eat buffet at the development stage of your novel. Eat too much and you'll feel bloated, the story will become a stagnated checklist that will lead to boredom and eventually abandonment of the idea. Eat too little and you'll still be hungry and needing to supplement yourself more. This will lead to you missing opportunities to develop your story and give your reader a realistic wow factor where they can't picture themselves in your protagonist's shoes. Find the balance in between these two extremes and you have a nice, well rounded hearty meal that your readers and you as an author can really sink your teeth into and enjoy. Bon Appetit.

Until next time, write on.

JR

Dialogue - It's Just All Talk Isn't It?

Dialogue is an essential part to storytelling. You can tell a lot by how a person talks, the language they use, the slang words included in the conversation and their reactions to what others say to them or about them.

Dialogue or conversations if you prefer, can often lead your story to progress at a faster or slower pace. Short snappy one word answers. Quick exchanges of questions and answers. An argument. All of these can lead to the pace of the story being fast. Likewise, long descriptive monologues can slow the story down.

There has to be peaks and troughs when writing an engaging storyline. You can't continuously run at 100mph all the time. Likewise, if you have an old man who is telling their story in monotonous monologue form for five pages, you're going to bore your reader and they will close the book.

I liken writing dialogue to a thunderstorm. You have the anticipation before, the slow build-up, rain pattering on the window before the clouds gather and you get the forks of lightning and then the clap of thunder overhead. The storm gathers momentum until it rages with all of its might and then leaves a calmness in its wake with a clear open sky. If you don't have ups and downs, rights and wrongs, good versus evil, argumentative versus placid, your dialogue will struggle to grip the reader's attention.

In real life conversations, our voices change tone. We can be aggressive, emotional, happy, sad, angry or calm and it is important that these things are addressed as all of these emotions and feelings can be expressed through dialogue. After all, you can't physically see the person like you would in real life or on TV so their body language is difficult to convey without changing the tone and structure of the sentences to show how they are feeling at that time.

How a person reacts in any given situation can add new dimensions to your characters. If they're angry, they will likely be giving short, sharp, aggressive answers. Words may become hyphenated or abbreviated as they aim to get the words out as fast as possible. Ain't, Don't, Feelin', Can't, Lovin', Know-It-All, etc.

If they're upset, you'll have the longer, drawn out answers with half complete sentences that get lost in their emotion. "I can't believe you did...." "What were you thinking? If only I..."

If they're calm and composed, you'll find words are articulated clearer and more precisely than if they were arguing. "I appreciate your concern." "Whatever happened here?"

However you structure your dialogue, the way your characters interact and speak to each other as well as their own internal voice are vital ingredients towards your reader having a deeper understanding and connection to who they are. Strong dialogue can take the reader and your characters to places that pages of description can only scrape the surface of. If you want to walk the walk, let your characters talk the talk.

Until next time, write on.

JR

Taboo Subjects And Political Correctness - Are We Taking Things Too Far?

We've all done it haven't we? That foot in mouth moment that we cringe about every time we think of it. That brief lapse of concentration when we let words escape our mouths when really they should have just stayed in our head instead. But has political correctness gone too far? Are we obsessed with being offended for the sake of being offended? And where will it end? Should we be worried and have to consider every word we say before we say it? And if so, what kind of world are we living in today?

There are some subjects which are considered taboo and for good reason. Throughout history women, children and people of different origins, sexes and backgrounds have been subjected to horrific discrimination through racism, sexism and abuse. These subjects are justifiably unacceptable in today's society, yet historically, they still create a bias that seems to seep through into today's world despite our best intentions. However, there is an argument of whether political correctness has gone too far.

I recently watched an old episode of the British comedy "Only Fools And Horses" which was apparently edited for outdated views and content. This was a product of a different generation and to censor things for outdated views and content leads to a whole new generation being unable to make decisions for themselves about what is right or wrong. Likewise, the James Bond films of the 1960's and 1970's have recently come under fire from people who believe that the character of James Bond was a sexist, misogynistic, arrogant and overly aggressive character in those films.

There are some scenes in the film, Goldfinger in particular, where Bond is receiving a massage and when Felix turns up he tells the young lady to leave because it's time for "man talk" and smacks her bum as she leaves. Likewise, when engaging in a judo fight with Pussy Galore in the barn later in the same film, it can be seen that Bond forced himself onto

Pussy without her initial consent. In today's world, both of these acts would see men brought to account for sexism and potentially sexual assault but how can erasing everything from the past help our future selves make the right decision? These films were a product of their time. Outdated? Yes. Sexist? Yes. But in today's world where we have millions of TV channels and streaming services at our fingertips, do we have to watch the films that we disagree with? No, we have freedom of choice for a reason.

So, whilst I do not condone the acts from the past, I also don't see who should be nominated as the judge and jury of what gets erased from history and what doesn't. If you don't like a book, film, TV series or whatever other media you engage with, you turn it off. You close the book. As humans we have evolved to learn from the mistakes of the past. To simply erase those mistakes so that future generations do not witness them is immoral and can lead to a dangerous precedent being made. How long before everything you say, see and do has to go through a censor before it is deemed to be allowed? And who makes that decision.

The same thing can begin to seep into the writing of your novels. If you write a historical piece, would you remove any scenes from that storyline in case it offends a reader even though it was proven to be a part of everyday life in say, Victorian Britain for example? Would it devalue your work if it was or was not included?

Novels and stories are the imagination and inspiration of the authors from whatever time they were written. From Shakespeare to the modern day classics, it all started from an individual's initial imagination of an idea they had at the time. This can often lead to their work becoming dated. A novel is dated from the day it is published. No one else would have come up with that idea on that particular day, at that particular time, in that particular way and in some cases, things change. Morals change. Outlooks change. Sometimes good, sometimes bad. Sometimes we need to be censored to save ourselves from ourselves but to completely erase any kind of historical text because it doesn't fit a modern day agenda is simply ludicrous. A story is a concept of its time, warts and all. If you don't like it, close the book. Read something else. But don't let ego get in the way of allowing people to learn from past mistakes.

Until next time, write on.

JR

Social Media; Friend Or Foe?

How many of us check our social media profiles everyday? How many of us respond consistently to the beeps, vibrates and pings whenever they occur? How many of us feel that more people are likely to read our social media posts than our books? Unfortunately, with the onset of the internet and the ability to have an electronic encyclopaedia in your pocket known as Google, our attention spans are becoming shorter and shorter.

So, what's the point of spending months, sometimes years, writing a 300+ page novel if nobody is going to read it? Surely it would be better to update social media every hour with cute photos of kittens and selfies hashtagged with "living my best life" whilst hiding the train wreck of my life behind a series of filters. Aren't we meant to give the people what they want?

Well, yes, modern technology has turned the majority of us into phone zombies who can barely go ten minutes without responding to that little dictator in our pockets but there is hope. The constant fear of missing out or FOMO as its acronym has become widely known, means that we are seeing mental health conditions becoming more and more apparent. Anxiety is at an all time high and employers are seeing hours upon hours of productivity lost in the workplace due to workers addiction to their phones. This rumbling volcano is bound to erupt sometime isn't it?

It already has. People are beginning to realise that there is more to life than staring at a screen for 8 hours per day. (Check your screen time, you'll be surprised how quickly it adds up!) Just like when we go to the cinema to see the latest films, more and more people are looking for escapism. A way to escape this relentless 24/7 on the go lifestyle that the 21st century demands of us. We are realising that occasionally, our bodies need time to recharge, to calm down and relax and there are few better ways to do this than with a good book.

More and more people are turning to novels to disappear into the minds and worlds of their favourite characters as they heroically save the day in whatever scenario they find themselves in. Sometimes it's fun, scary, emotional, adventurous, twisted, mysterious, whatever genre we enjoy, most of all, it is an opportunity to connect to a life outside of our own. A moment of fantasy, of escapism and joy. From the days of cavemen and women gathering around the fire through to the instantly downloaded ebook on your tablet, storytelling is what unites us all whatever media we read it through.

So, is social media a friend or foe? It can be both. A lot of the time, it is a distraction from what we are attempting to achieve in our day; however, used correctly, it can be an amazing marketing tool for up-and-coming authors to advertise their work to potential readers. The theft of the reader's attention can also be the gateway into gaining their attention so, as much as you want your readers to only engage with your story, don't dismiss the power of advertisements to complete the full circle. After all, how did your readers discover your book in the first place?

Until next time, write on.

JR

Are Writing Courses Worth Your Time?

A lot of people ask how do I become an author? Where do you get your ideas from? I tend to give them the same answer. Anybody can become an author. Whether you're 18 or 80, you have a story within you that needs to be told. All you need to do is to allow the words to flow from your mind onto the paper or screen. Everyone around us is living their own lives. They are the lead character in their own life story. Everyone around them, everyone they encounter on a daily basis, from the waitress in the coffee shop, the bus driver, their office colleagues, their boss, they all have their own stories, troubles, thoughts, feelings, fears and emotions.

Then I stumbled across the BBC Maestro series which included two writing courses by my favourite authors Harlan Coben and Lee Child. Being so focused on writing my own novels and short stories, I dismissed the idea of a writing course as it seemed to be taking me away from what I wanted to do, which was to write. How wrong I was. When there was a special offer on the courses just before Christmas, I decided to give it a try and have been hooked ever since. The amount of knowledge, experience, inspiration and guidance in these two courses alone made it worth the subscription fee. Most writers would have read hundreds of books in their lifetime and from that, you would have understood the structure, the plotting and the flow of writing a book from the genre you like. These courses go further in depth and afterwards you realise that what they were telling you, you already knew but failed to acknowledge it. It was like opening the author's eyes and making them realise that there is no supernatural power behind it. Anyone can write, all you need to do is to pay attention to everyone and everything around you. Write the story that you would want to read is the mantra and it is true.

So, are writing courses worth your time? You need to find one that will give you what you need in regards to what your new writing project is about. For me, writing crime thrillers, the BBC Maestro courses were perfect but likewise, if you were writing a film script, a TV series or theatrical play for example, you are better off targeting courses that deal with that specific area. You can read all of the "how to" books and listen to all of the podcasts you can find but the most important part of making a writing course work for you is to write.

My misconception that taking these courses would prevent me from writing has actually had the opposite effect, I'm writing more than ever! Let your words flow no matter how outrageous they may seem. You can always edit it later however, it is impossible to edit a blank page. Sometimes, you just need to let go of that hyper-critical editor in your head. Save them for later when you're perfecting your second/third/fourth draft. Initially, just let it flow and you'll be surprised by the results.

Foolishly, I thought that I'd learn nothing from writing courses and that they were just a distraction from completing my work-in-progress and moving onto the next project. I'm happy to say that I was wrong. You never stop learning. When I look back at my first attempts, I can see so many things that, if I were to embark on that project again, I would do things significantly differently to how it was done back then. If a writing course can help you broaden your knowledge and improve your craft then I would definitely recommend the investment. For me, it was worth it and I'm looking forward to devouring as many courses as I can in the next 12 months.

Until next time, write on.

JR

How Complicated Is Too Complicated If You Complicate A Complicated Plot With Too Much Complication?

Confused? So am I. And that is what you want to prevent when you write your novel. We have all seen films, soap operas, TV dramas, they all have lots of characters populating their scenes. The problem with reading a novel, short story or even at times a screenplay is, the reader only has a certain amount of absorption in your plot and storyline.

As an author, you may know that your 27th character is Aunt Bette from the hairdressers who is a man-eating, overindulging, mutton-dressed-as-lamb, gold-digger who loves nothing more than sushi and hot-tubbing. The problem is, your readers will be constantly flicking back through the pages trying to keep track of who is who, leading to them eventually becoming confused and giving up on your novel altogether.

Novels such as thrillers and mysteries have an element of confusion within them to keep the reader guessing until the end. Many stories go off on tangents earlier in the novel which either reappear later as a vital clue or are just red herrings leading the reader's mind elsewhere. This is confusion of plot rather than confusion caused by complication. When you confuse by complication, you are frustrating your reader with too much "filler" content and not getting straight to the point.

The same can be said for so-called "info-dumps" in your novel. If you've set your novel in London for example but have never visited, you may have been doing extensive research online to gain knowledge of how people who visit or live in London experience things. The transport system, Buckingham Palace, The London Eye, The Houses Of Parliament etc. The reader doesn't need to know every minute detail of your protagonist's visit to London and everything they saw along the way.

Here is where less is more comes into play. You are overcomplicating the plot with an info-dump of walking over Westminster Bridge with the London Eye on your right and seeing Big Ben and trawling the markets on your way to Waterloo Station which by the way has a clock in the middle where couples like to meet... Stop! You don't need all that. Simply saying that your protagonist walked across the bridge and noticed the lights of the London Eye reflecting across the river will give the reader enough for their imagination to fill in the blanks.

Falling in love with your hero or heroine can also lead to further complications. If you are adamant that your protagonist has to look a very specific way, always dress a certain way, always react the same way in certain circumstances, you are overcomplicating the world in which your character's live. People change their minds constantly. There is generally very few occasions where consistency is key. The readers pick up your book for an element of escapism and part of that escapism is to imagine in their own mind what the main character looks like. Of course you would want to give basic details, hair colour, build, possibly their age, but don't overcompensate or overcomplicate things to the point that the reader has no input.

Let them fill in the blanks for themselves. After all, what's more important, your vision of your hero or the readers? Don't overcomplicate things for the sake of complication. You want to keep your readers engaged from the first to the last page, don't turn them off midway through.

A great quote that always sticks with me when I try to simplify things; "The first chapter sells this book, the last chapter sells the next one." Don't lose your reader along the way. They came on this journey with you for a reason, you can still make your writing intriguing, authentic and gripping without creating unnecessary speed bumps along the way. The smoother the ride, the less chance complication has of overcomplicating your already complicated plot.

Until next time, write on.
JR

Is It Important To Plot Your Entire Book In Advance?

As a writer, I get asked these questions a lot. Is it important to plot your entire book in advance? How do you plot your storylines and bring them all together at the end? Do you have to know every detail of the story before you write it? I know some writers that do but for me, I plan very little of my stories in advance with the view that it will come to me as I write. From the first sentence to the last, I have no idea what is going to happen to get from A to B. The characters seem to take on a life of their own and I'm there furiously writing about what they are doing as the story progresses.

Let me explain, spoiler alert, if you haven't read The Blake Langford Adventures yet, go away and read them before carrying on here. I usually have an idea of what I would like to happen in a story but very little development happens until I begin writing. For a story such as Where No One Stands Alone, my first Blake Langford adventure, it was going to be a love story about Blake being reunited with his fiance, Rachael, who disappeared 8 years ago. That was all I had when it started out. It ended up being an adventure involving diamond smuggling and murder which started out in Italy in 1999 and then spread via London, Miami and Mexico. Was Blake going to be reunited with his fiance in the end? Partly yes, they did see each other again but this storyline began to create new ideas for adventures in the future so the happy ending turned out to be of a different kind which continues through the rest of the series.

If I had meticulously planned this storyline out, Rachael and Blake would have been reunited and that would be the end of the series tied up in a paint-by-numbers way that may well have ended up boring the readers. There would have been no room to explore the adventures of the other characters and how their actions in turn would affect the plot or any future storylines. I find that by simply having a start and finish point with little or no plans in between, it allows me to have creative ideas as the story progresses. So, does it always go to plan? To be honest, no. Sometimes I tend to go down rabbit holes and the story comes to a grinding halt. That's the joy of having a first draft that can be edited over and over again. You can make these mistakes and then, if needed, take a few steps back and turn right instead of left at a certain point and have a different ending. I've always had the mindset that it is easier to edit 30 pages that went in the wrong direction than a blank page of procrastination and fear of failure.

The open-ended conclusion of Where No One Stands Alone led into the second book in the series, Underneath The Covers, becoming a sequel to the first book. Again, very little planning went into this book. At the time, I had recently visited Edinburgh, in Scotland, with my family for a few days as a city break to see the sights. Looking up at the huge Edinburgh Castle and seeing the dungeons gave me an idea of where Blake needed to go next. He was still reeling from the loss of Rachael at the end of the first book but now he had the new responsibilities of being a father but he still needed closure. Being able to explore other characters in Where No One Stands Alone, allowed me to reintroduce some of the characters in Underneath The Covers and in a way, continue the saga from the first book but in completely new surroundings. The readers enjoyed the first book so it was a case of bringing a similar but different formula to book 2. The only planning for Underneath The Covers was that I'd like to set it in Edinburgh, Blake struggles to balance his personal and professional life after grieving Rachael's loss and he needed closure on the people who betrayed him in Mexico. From that came a plan to steal jewels from Holyrood Palace, the Royal Family's residence in Scotland, murders in the castle and a high speed boat and helicopter chase in the north sea. Again, don't let your original plan make you believe that there is only one way for your story to go. Be brave and take the path you least expect to work and see how it goes.

So, my thoughts on planning a novel, yes, you do need a rough idea of who your characters are and what their objective is, however, don't trap yourself into a corner. Don't restrict yourself with a rigid idea that you had 2 years ago and it has to be done that way with no wriggle room. The best stories that I find interesting are the ones where I don't know what happens next. I'm experiencing it as I'm writing in the same way that your reader will experience it on the first time they read it. After all, nothing in real life goes to plan. Very few things stay the same and nothing is predictable. You always need to go into your writing with a "what if?" question hanging over every scenario. Most of the time you will have at least three different ways that you can tackle a storyline, whether you choose A, B or C is up to you, but make sure you're fully invested in it and you enjoy the process. If you enjoy it, there's a good chance your readers will too.

Until next time, write on.

JR

How Important Is It To Take Your Reader Out Of Everyday Life With Extraordinary Characters In A Changing World?

When you stare at the blank screen in front of you, willing the words to come through to create your next novel or short story, the one focus that should remain front and centre throughout your creation is your reader. After all, if nobody reads your work, are you a successful writer?

A lot of the advice that new writers receive is to write for a certain genre of readers but trying to please everybody will lead you to create a mediocre mess that will please nobody. We are all very similar as humans and you will generally find that the books you personally enjoy reading, will heavily influence the books you end up writing for others. If you enjoy a certain genre or series, the chances are someone else will too. If you read a book and think to yourself, "I could have written something better/as good as this," now is the time to prove it. But how much does an author need to focus on his/her/their readers? How much do we need to take them out of everyday life and into the lives of the characters we create in fiction? The answer lies in the suspension of belief and of everyday constraints. After all, how many of the characters in modern fiction will be struggling to pay their bills each month, vegging out in front of the TV with a share size bag of Doritos and ten cans of lager? Or how many will be dutifully completing their housework, walking their dogs, tidying up the kids' bedrooms or shouting at the idiot causing a traffic jam on the morning commute to work. Very few.

Readers tend to pick up a book for a moment of relaxation. Maybe to read a couple of chapters before bed, to pass the time on a commute or even to read on their break at work. The things these scenarios and many others have in common are knowledge and escapism. Some people will read self-help books, educational literature, almost anything to help them learn about how to improve themselves, their well-being or to improve their chances for a promotion at work or maybe training towards a new job. Others are just looking for an escape from their daily lives. To dream of a world a million miles away from where they currently are. A world where the daily mundane cycle of life doesn't exist and the reader can escape there for a while. That is where a fiction writer can make or break a relationship with their potential reader.

We are all caught in the hamster wheel of life and with remote working becoming more popular and with the reliance on social media to keep in touch with people, we are becoming more lonely, isolated and depressed than ever. With the advance of the internet, shops, cafes, pubs and bars are closing down all over the country. This is leading to less and less social opportunities for people to have real life conversations and connections. For a lot of people, the latest updates on their social media feed tend to be their only knowledge of an outside world that is becoming less and less social.

So, how do authors take advantage of this situation and help their readers firstly discover their work and secondly, take the chance on their new novel and transport themselves into this new fantasy world?

With the digitalisation that has happened in the past twenty years, we have come a long way from storytelling around the campfire. Streaming services, DVD's, films and TV series are all striving to grab the attention of people as they plague their devices with advertisements and special offers to gain their attention. As an author, it is your responsibility to make the difference. You may not have the million dollar/pound budgets that the big companies have but in your 300 or so pages of prose, you have the opportunity to distract, delight, intrigue, question, surprise and humour your reader. Done well, this will keep your reader coming back again and again. If you create a series, the baseline is already there. If they know your consistent recurring character is going to return in new surroundings and scenarios, chances are, you are going to hook your reader and leave them wanting more.

Is it important to take your reader out of everyday life with extraordinary characters in a changing world? Absolutely. You have the chance to make a difference in someone else's life through the words you create on the page. Surely you'd want to do that wouldn't you?

Until next time, write on.

JR

So, You Want To Write A Series...

Some writers enjoy the freedom of standalone novels and short stories. The ability to change your characters, places, scenarios, practically anything and everything from one novel to the next. And then we have the series writers. We all enjoy series whether it be Jack Reacher, James Bond, Poirot, Morse, Miss Marple or any that you can mention. Readers can often prefer stories that are contained in a series because they already have an idea of what they are getting.

Using Lee Child's Jack Reacher series as an example. You know Reacher is going to be a loner travelling from town to town across the United States helping those in need and dispatching the bad guys. It's the same formula each time but different. And different is the key here. You wouldn't necessarily read the same book twenty times yet you'll read twenty different Reacher novels with the same structure, the same through line and the same result.

TV, streaming services, films and even podcasts now compete for the attention of those who read novels and give them several options for the escapism they crave. What is going to make them pick up your book rather than their phone/tablet or TV remote? The answer, a consistent, thrilling, adventurous, intriguing story. Whatever media you consume, whether it be a TV series, film or book, the key is the same, give the people what they want, make them want to know more and keep them interested from start to finish.

So, by that margin, if every writer thought that they needed to write the most incredible, best ever prose of their life every time they opened their laptop or picked up their pen, would they even start? The millions of books, stories and films out there tell us a resounding yes! But don't let intimidation stop you from entering this world. Nobody ever publishes their first draft! Especially when writing a series, consistency is key. You need to know your world and your characters inside-out. To do that, you need to do two things; firstly, write with complete faith that your organic storytelling will come from your subconscious. A combination of the life you have led, the books you've read, the films you've watched and the stories you've heard from others throughout your life. All of this will be amalgamated into your first draft. Secondly; edit.

That second point is intentionally vague. If you want to work in a series, you need to edit like this world you have created is happening around you right now. You know the name of every character, their appearance, their quirks, their smell, what they had for breakfast, their pet's name, their family relations, their secrets, and then as everything happens around them, you write it down in as much detail as possible leaving no stone unturned. When you've encapsulated this world, edit, edit and edit some more. Keep the world consistent, make sure every character is distinct enough that you automatically know who is talking, how they will express themselves and how they will react in any given situation. Only then, will you be able to create the confidence that the reader needs to trust that this series is worth their time, effort and money. In a world full of a million distractions, you need to make sure that you are at least in the top 10. The book that the reader will stay up until 4am reading just because they have to know the ending. They have to know what happened to the main protagonist, how the secondary stories are all tied up and what has been left for the reader to decide or for what could potentially be the next book in the series.

I often refer to the old BBC sitcom, "Only Fools And Horses" when discussing series writing. You knew that Del and Rodney were bound to get themselves into some kind of hilarious situation that almost always was going to end badly and this comes to the same but different point that I made earlier. You always knew that Del would have bought some dodgy merchandise that he would make Rodney go and sell down the market, mostly to his own detriment, yet there was still enough expansion, improvement and diversion of storylines to withstand 64 episodes of the sitcom. Regular subtle changes to scenarios, building on the character arcs made the series engaging and this is what you need to achieve if you plan to write a series of books. Learn from previous storylines. What worked. What didn't and why? Keep the stories unique but based in the same formula and you have the chance to make your series a success.

Taking my own series of books into account, the adult fiction series, The Blake Langford Adventures, has now run into three full novels with a fourth due out later this year. Despite Blake being an agent of Special Branch and travelling all over the world, he still has a family unit at the heart of the storyline and this dynamic is repeated throughout the series. In the children's series; The New Adventures Of Cornelius Cone And Friends, that I co-write with my friend, Steve Boyce; Cornelius and his friends are based in the community of Hythe Village. Throughout the storylines, Cornelius and his friend, Bennie Barrier, often engage with the locals such as Tricia Trolley, Postman Pete and Trevor Traffic Light as they go on their adventures and this community holds the series together and makes each character accountable for their own actions. This year, I have now released another children's series; Bennie Barrier's Big City Adventures, where Cornelius Cone's friend Bennie decides to move out of the village to live in Southampton city centre. After a tricky start where he is unwelcome by the city Maintenance Team, Bennie works on building up his friendship circle and working on his initiative to earn his place in the new city Maintenance Team. Again, we come back to the "same but different" scenario where taking Bennie Barrier out of Cornelius Cone's world could have worked against the series but it has now created a new series to run and sometimes overlap with the original Cornelius Cone adventures. Consistency is key and if you can find a way to keep your readers coming back for more, you're on to a winner!

Until next time, write on.

JR

How Important Is It That The Author Is 100% Happy With Their Book?

If you're an author, you're already aware of the need for your work to be read by people who enjoy the genre you write in. After all, you wouldn't have decided to become an author at all if you hadn't read your fair share of books in the genre you write in. There is a good chance that several books that you have enjoyed in the past have influenced how you approach your current and future writing projects.

You know what worked for you in those novels. You also know what didn't work for you too. And that leads us on to the question, how important is it that the author is 100% happy with their book?

We often hear the phrase, "fake it until you make it." That doesn't apply when you're spending months, sometimes years, honing, editing, perfecting the manuscript for your current/next novel. You will have spent hundreds, sometimes thousands of hours creating that initial idea, that first draft and several re-writes of that same story to make it the best it can be. If you can't stand the sight of what you have written. If you're not interested, intrigued or engaged with what you are writing, it will stand out like a sore thumb. If you hate what you're reading, the chances are, your reader will too.

A lot of people believe that getting your work noticed and into the hands of people who want to read it is like solving a rubix cube. There's some huge complicated method that only certain individuals know. Many years ago, traditional publishers and agents were the gatekeepers to the industry. To get past first base, you had to produce something extraordinary that appealed to the agent before it went anywhere near the publishing house. Then, along came the internet and with it, the opportunity to put yourself out into the world like never before. Blogs, videos, social media, podcasts, your own website; creatives have never had it so good. So why was there a stigma around Self Publishing?

For a long time, self publishing was the black sheep of the family. The drivel that anyone could type out onto a word document that would be published with no questions asked often leading to books that were of substandard quality in terms of look and content. With the advancement of AI, people looking to make money fast have been trying to flood the market with algorithms where they give the AI and initial prompt and expect it to write a 60,000 word, 250 page novel for them instantly. This has catastrophically failed. Maybe in the future, the AI programs such as ChatGPT, Sudowrite or any of the others on the market may have the ability to write prose good enough to last for a full length novel but there is one thing that AI does not have, the human touch. Every story/novel you have ever read had a human with emotions, challenges, needs and ambition behind every story. No matter what AI can come up with, it cannot fake human emotion.

And that is why the author should be 100% happy before sending their book out into the world. Of course, editors will have their say of what they recommend to improve your first draft. Ironing out inconsistencies, grammar and punctuation along the way but the core story should still belong to the author. If you let your editor change a significant percentage of your story, is it still your story? I'm not saying that you should disregard the advice of your editor and publisher but in the end, the work that has your name attached to it is still yours. Whether you sell 1 copy of 1 million copies, the storyline is yours and you need to own it 100%.

Until next time, write on.

JR

Hollywood Wants To Turn My Novel Into A Movie... But They Want To Change 90% Of It! What Happened To My Novel?

It's the moment that most writers dream about. The moment that Hollywood comes knocking at their door and tells them they want to make their novel into a movie with a huge cheque for the rights. Excitement builds as the details of huge sets being built, famous actors and actresses are interested in the key parts and you finally have the opportunity to see your masterpiece on the big screen and then.... You suddenly realise that 90% of your storyline has been disregarded by the screenwriters, directors and producers and you're left staring at a cast of characters and a plot that barely acknowledges the 70k words you tirelessly spent writing in your novel. So, you're left asking the question; "What happened to my novel?"

The honest answer is nothing. Your novel still exists. Your original storyline still exists. Your loyal readers who praise your prose every time you release a new book still exist. And that huge cheque is in your hands just waiting to be cashed. A brutal assessment? Probably, but the reality is, very often in television and film, a cast of screenwriters will agonise over a story or script and will often change it hundreds of times until the dialogue feels comfortable, not only to them, but also to the actors and actresses playing the part.

We've all read books or watched films that don't quite resonate with us. Sometimes we'll even close the book or turn off the film and never revisit it again. It may be that the film appeals to the vast majority of people but for whatever reason, it just didn't hit the spot for us and that's okay. If we all liked the same things, looked the same and acted the same, the world would be a pretty boring place to be. The same can be said for a novel that gets made into a film. For whatever reason, a scene, a chapter, even a whole section of the novel may not sit right with the screenwriters, directors, producers or actors/actresses. As a writer, you would struggle to write a novel that you were not 100% invested in and likewise, the film crew would struggle to make the film the best it could be if they were not 100% invested in it either.

That by no means discredits you as an author of that story. Personal preferences can often make or break the success or failure of a book or film project and often, previous films and books are revisited with fresh eyes, fresh ideas and the remake will often go on to be a major success in the future. The reason that this storyline exists is because you, the author, put that storyline, those characters and those scenarios out into the world and your loyal readers will continue to enjoy it for years to come. Your book will not disappear if Hollywood decides to make a film of it. If anything, it will generate a whole new spectre of advertising and may bring a whole new crowd of people to read your books. So don't get too hung up on the nuts and bolts of the story and if it will appear as you thought it would on the big screen. You've made your commitment to getting your book out there and by doing that, you are a long way ahead of those who want to write a book but have yet to type or write the first word. As Don Williams once said; "If Hollywood don't need you, honey I still do." Don't let the lure of fame stop you from being the writer you always knew you could be. The money is nice to have but being true to your creativity, that's something special.

Until next time, write on.

JR

I've Published My Book And Only Sold 1 Copy...

This is a comment that I see so often on social media as the ability to get your work out into the world becomes easier, the competition to actually sell your work becomes a lot harder. With the advance in Artificial Intelligence, some people are coming up with initial ideas, placing them into an AI algorithm and expecting it to produce a novel. They then upload this document, unchecked, unedited, to a self publishing company and flood the market. This, in turn, leads to a saturated market of substandard content that gives self publishers the reputation of putting any old rubbish out into the world and to hell with the consequences. Thankfully, companies such as Amazon KDP have noticed this trend and have now put things in place to prevent this happening in the future. So, if this is the case, why have so many self published authors only sold 1 copy of their book?

Despite the flood of AI generated material, a lot of indie authors out there are producing better and better books as they learn their craft, become better at constructing a storyline that flows, is imaginative, has an original feel to it and has the fundamental building blocks to be a success. After all, to be a successful author, you need to be a successful reader. To gain the enthusiasm to write, you must at some point have read a book and thought, I could do this. We're all products of our environment. Whether you realise it or not, the media you consume, the people you meet, the places that you go, they will all influence your writing in one way or another. Most characters in your storyline would in some way be similar to someone you know or a favourite character in a TV series, film or book.

The problem a lot of indie authors have is, no matter how good their book is, if people don't know it exists, how are they meant to be able to buy it? A lot of authors get put off by the big publishing houses and by agents turning down their manuscripts and therefore, decide to go it alone and self publish. Unfortunately, like any business, publishing houses need to make money. They have the financial clout to advertise their books in newspapers, on TV, online, on huge billboards across the cities of the world but in the end, it all comes down to how much money they can generate from the sales of their books. If a famous celebrity writes an average novel at the same time an indie author writes an absolute thriller of a novel, chances are, the publishing house would go with the celebrity rather than the indie author. The reason being, the celebrity already has a following and can command huge sales based purely on their popularity in the media they work in.

Whilst this may seem unfair, again, the publishing house is a business. It stands to make more money from the celebrity than taking a risk on the new author. If you went to the betting shop on cup final day and Manchester United were playing a non-league team, you wouldn't necessarily bet thousands of pounds on the non-league team winning the cup final would you? That's not to say that it is impossible for the non-league team to beat the mighty Manchester United but it is highly unlikely that you would get a return on your investment. The same gamble is taken every time a publishing house releases a new book. It has invested several thousand pounds/dollars into this book release, it needs to at least recoup that money and then make a profit.

So, how can indie authors level the playing field? Exposure. Social media, YouTube, TikTok, they all have allowed us to present ourselves to the world in ways we have never been able to before. Is your Facebook or Twitter/X profile been laying dormant with holiday snaps from 10 years ago on it. Make it work for you. Advertise your books. Appear on podcasts. Do you have a smart phone? Why not make a short video of yourself advertising your books and post it on TikTok or YouTube? And make sure you connect with others. There must be some give and take online if you aim to build up a community around you and your projects. It can't all be take, take, take. Share someone else's promotions. Like other people's status's and advertisements. Comment and offer your own feedback on what you think they are doing right and wrong. Most of all, build your own brand. Let the world know that you exist because how can they buy your book if you don't tell them that it exists? Stand out in the crowd! Over a million people in this space? Be that one in a million that makes it! Believe in yourself and you'll be amazed at what you can achieve.

Until next time, write on.

JR

Do You Look At The Man/Woman In The Street And Wonder... What's Their Story? If So, They Could Be The Inspiration You Need For Your Next Book!

As an author, I tend to find inspiration in the strangest of places but if you're struggling to find the niche that you're looking for, the answer could be right in front of you.

When you go to the supermarket to do your weekly shopping, have you ever noticed the elderly lady carefully selecting her loaf of bread? The 20 year old buying his alcohol? The parent looking at the children's biscuits? The checkout worker who looks like he/she would rather be anywhere else but where he/she is today? We've all seen these people but do you ever wonder what their story may be?

The elderly lady may have been a dancer, a doctor, a solicitor or maybe even an office worker in her younger days. How many children did she have, if any? What places has she visited during her lifetime? What hobbies does she have? Has she been involved in anything extraordinary in her life? Does she have a husband? Is she a widow? All of these questions can start to build up a character profile which could be used in your novel.

Basing characters on real life people can often help you as an author to produce well rounded characters that your readers can engage with. Of course, you should not create a character that can easily be identified as someone you know without their permission but creative licence can mean that you can take some parts of one person, some parts of another and mould them together to create your fictional character.

I used to work with two men who regularly had farting and belching competitions in the workplace. This gave me the inspiration for Bertie Bin, one of the characters in the children's series that I co-wrote with my friend Steve Boyce called The New Adventures Of Cornelius Cone And Friends. Bertie Bin lives in Bluebell Park and works alongside Bella Bin and Rita Red Bin to keep the park clean and tidy.

Bella Bin handles all of the recycling, Rita Red Bin collects all of the dog poo bags and Bertie Bin will eat anything he can find therefore leading to him having poor hygiene and regular bouts of flatulence. The combination of two of my former work colleagues made Bertie Bin a loveable, albeit at times, vulgar character in the series, often with humorous results.

So, when you next pass someone in the street, it can be worth noting their appearance and allow your imagination to run wild. What would they do in various circumstances? Where do they work? What is their past? What ambitions do they have for the future? You'll be amazed by how many scenarios can be created just by letting your imagination fill in the gaps. You may be right, you may be completely wrong but if you're writing fiction, creating extraordinary characters is part of the fun.

Until next time, write on.

JR

I'm 40 Years Old, What Do I Know About Writing For Children?

During the pandemic, we all had extra time on our hands to do the things we'd been putting off for years. Becoming a father gives you the chance to relive parts of your childhood alongside your children and reading books is a big part of that. As I was reading stories to my son, we began talking about all of the different ways the story could end. What would potentially happen after the story and if those events could make a new story alongside the one we were reading.

At the time, my friend Steve Boyce had recently wrote a children's book called Cornelius Cone And Friends about a traffic cone who worked in the local area. When I discussed our ideas with him, Steve offered me the chance to write my own Cornelius Cone adventures alongside his original version. I had always enjoyed writing from a young age but this gave me the platform to explore my ideas and writing for the first time in many years. The problem I had was, I'm almost 40, how do I know what works for a children's story in today's world?

The answer can be found in revisiting your childhood and engaging with children in the age group you are writing for. Cornelius Cone is aimed at Primary School children so what are their wants, needs, concerns and interests? Does the story need to be dramatic, humorous, mysterious, scary or maybe even a bit silly? Over 80 ebook adventures, we tried to encapsulate all of that. Used examples of real life characters, local landmarks and explored the world from a child's point of view.

Walking through the supermarket and seeing a wet floor sign and thinking, if that sign came to life, what would it do? Who would it speak to? How would it act? This created the character called Wet Floor, always worrying that he won't be in the right place at the right time, friends with Tricia Trolley and always rushing around to get his jobs done as quickly as possible.

When visiting the park, we noticed three bins near to the picnic bench, one for general waste, one for recycling and one for dog waste. These three bins turned out to be Bertie Bin, Bella Bin and Rita Red Bin. Rita would only eat dog waste and would often need some mints for her breath. Bella would only eat recyclable plastic, paper and cans whilst Bertie Bin would eat anything he could get his hands on and would suffer the consequences of it later.

If you can embrace the childlike view of the world combined with the items and people that you see around you, even at 40, you can still build a world where children can engage, interact and enjoy. The Harry Potter series is a prime example of this but in Cornelius Cone's world, we tried to keep it a little more simple but who knows where it might lead? If you'd like to find out more about Cornelius Cone, please visit www.CorneliusCone.co.uk[1]

Until next time, write on.

JR

1. http://www.corneliuscone.co.uk

How Soon Should I Introduce My Main Protagonist?

A common mistake that new authors make is delaying the introduction of their main protagonist into their story. They tend to prioritise scene building and other aspects of the plot but, in order for your reader to care about what happens in your story, they need a character that they can immediately identify with.

You could have the most spectacular opening scene. A dramatic car chase, an explosion, some kind of end of the world doomsday scenario playing out, but if your reader doesn't connect with your main protagonist until several pages into the novel, you've lost that immediate connection and potentially, your reader.

When you begin your novel, you should aim to start your story at a point of conflict or somewhere where the reader is immediately drawn into what's happening. Look at the two examples below;

1. "The snow covered mountains, like icing on a Christmas cake, created a looming shadow over the village on a cold December morning as the villagers went about their daily chores."

1. "How do you know she was there?" Beth asked. "I saw her coming out of the house," John replied. "But she was meant to be in Plymouth." "I guess her plans changed."

The first paragraph is world building and creates a picture in the reader's mind but doesn't immediately pose a question. From a reader's point of view, you've created a Christmas scene and nothing more. They won't necessarily have the enthusiasm to continue from this point as there is no question in their mind of what happens next?

In the second paragraph, we're straight into the conversation. Questions are immediately posed to the reader. Who are Beth and John? Who are they talking about? Why is it so important that the person they are talking about isn't where they thought she was? Straightaway, your reader is engaged and wanting answers to the questions posed in the opening paragraph. They have potentially two characters they can cling onto as the main protagonists and they know that these two people will potentially be taking them through the story.

Sub-plots that run alongside your main story can add an extra dimension to your storyline with extra characters and scenarios, however, it is unwise to deviate from the characters that you have introduced at the start. If your reader thinks that, in this example, Beth and John are the main characters and then the story becomes about two completely different characters that are unrelated to Beth and John's story, they are less likely to care about the plight of any of the characters in the story.

Making that initial connection with the reader can be key to a novel's success. Think about when you visit a bookstore and are attracted by the cover of the book on the shelf. Most of us will pick it up, read the synopsis and perhaps read the first paragraph or two of the book before deciding whether to buy it or not. That synopsis and opening paragraph is your sales pitch. It is what decides whether someone will buy your book or not. It should be an advertisement for what your book is about and should hook the reader by making them want to find out more. Marketing your book is hard enough already, don't miss out on this valuable opportunity to draw your reader in.

Until next time, write on.

JR

Can You Over-Describe A Descriptive Piece Of Description That Describes The Descriptive Nature Of Your Novel?

Confused? So will your readers be too. Let's address the elephant in the room, the dreaded info-dumping. A lot of new authors when writing the first draft seem to overindulge in the details of their characters and scenes. The reality is, the reader doesn't need to know every intricate detail of your character's appearance, every tiny detail of where they live or even where they are going.

As an author, for continuity purposes, I tend to write out a character arc in a notebook for my own reference but when someone picks up your book, especially a work of fiction, they are looking for escapism. They're looking to use their imagination and leaving details deliberately vague is a good way to allow them to do this.

There are times when a character's backstory can be relevant to the storyline but these details need to be added sparingly and at the right time. Paragraphs of description and backstory can often bore the reader, slow down the pace of your novel and risk your reader giving up on the rest of the story. Seasoning your story, as if adding a condiment to your favourite food, should be done with care. Too much and you risk overpowering the flavour, not enough and it becomes bland.

Research is key if you want your novel to have a realistic feel in a world of your imagination. For example, without extensive research, you would struggle to write a novel set in London if you've lived your entire life in San Francisco and have never even visited London. A lot of writers can fall in love with their research. They end up with pages upon pages of notes and then endeavour to include pages upon pages of information into their story. This is a sure fire way to kill your narrative. Just because you have all of this information to hand, doesn't necessarily mean that every part of it has to be used.

When creating your character's world, only give the details that are necessary to advance your scene and keep things relevant. If your protagonist is walking down the street, we don't need to know how many houses there are, if there is a postbox, how many cars are parked outside but if there is a particular house where our protagonist is due to meet someone, we need to focus on a unique aspect of that particular house. Is it the only house with a red door? Or is it the only house with flower beds in the garden or maybe a rusted old metal gate where the others have new ones? Key details that are sprinkled in to colour the black and white world of your imagination can be the difference between making your story memorable or making it boring.

So, when creating memorable worlds and characters in your novel, less is often worth more. Avoid insulting your reader's intelligence by overexplaining yourself and allow them to fall into this world you have created, highlighted with their own imagination. If they can draw their own conclusions from your work, they are more likely to feel more involved in your world, have more emotion towards your characters and in turn, will enjoy your work a lot more. Being an author can be very rewarding when you are creating your story, but making a difference in a reader's life, that takes something special.

Until next time, write on.

JR

Does Every Chapter Need To End On A Cliffhanger?

When you stare at the blank page before you write your first word of your short story or novel, what do you aim to achieve? If the answer is, I want my readers to thoroughly enjoy my story, I want it to grip them, interest them and keep them turning the pages from start to finish and keep them guessing what happens next, then to do that, you need to have their full engagement in your characters, your storyline, the scenarios your characters find themselves in and the plot of your story.

Every story needs to have its own rhythm. If you read a story out loud and you stumble over words or it feels disjointed in some way, then the rhythm of the story is not flowing. Like a piece of music that is played by an orchestra, the conductor has the responsibility to keep all of the musicians in time. If one member of the orchestra is either out of time or playing a different piece of music to everyone else then as a collective, it just won't work.

The same can be said for writing a novel or a short story. As an author, you are the conductor of your own orchestra. You need to have control over every one of your characters in your story. How they talk, their reactions to different scenarios, how much of a risk taker they are. You should have an understanding of how your characters will react in any given circumstance. If you can do this, you stand more of a chance of encapsulating your reader and keeping them interested from start to finish.

Characters in your novel need to be bold. They need to be extroverted and larger than life. If you wrote about the mundane individual who works 40 hours per week in the same job, doing the same thing every day, meeting the same people, eating the same food, following the same routine day in, day out, your novel will quickly become boring and your reader will give up on it.

That's where the role of cliffhangers comes in. If you watch a TV series, each episode ends with a question or a cliffhanger that leads you to want to watch the next episode to find out what happens next. Your chapters are your episodes. Not every chapter needs to be dramatic and have pace pounding adrenaline from start to finish but it needs to pose an intriguing question. A question, that your reader at 1am, is compelled to read on and find out the answer to.

Intrigue is key to keeping people interested in your work. With the advance of social media and streaming services, it's become harder than ever to encourage people to pick up a book and read a full length novel. Social media keeps people glued to its feed because on every refresh, they will discover a new post, some new information. That is what your cliffhanger needs to do. You need to lead your reader into an intriguing plot, with characters they are interested in or can relate to and put them into extraordinary situations that makes the reader think; "What would I do in that situation?" If you can do that, you are well on your way to hooking your reader from start to finish and making your novel or short story an enjoyable and successful read.

Until next time, write on.

JR

Info-Dumping, How Can We Avoid It?

We've all seen it haven't we? That page and a half of unbroken text that gives you line and verse of a character from birth to present day and everything in between. As an author, it is essential that you know your characters inside out. That you can engage the reader in their world and know how they are likely to react in any given circumstance but does your reader have to know all of that? No.

Your reader will be visiting the world of your characters for a short time and capturing a snapshot of whatever scenario your short story or novel is set around. The information they need is minimal. Most people will read your book and look for a sense of escapism from the stresses and anxieties of the real world. It's their chance to be Cinderella at the ball or Jack Reacher beating the bad guys to pieces. But less is more.

The reader's imagination will fill in the blanks for things that are left intentionally vague. Your main character may be a 30-something man with black hair, muscular build and works for a law firm in the city and his name is Jason Harding. As he continues on his journey through the novel we will get to learn his mannerisms, characteristics, friendships, what matters to him, perhaps his personal relationships and family. That is about as much information as we are likely to need to build up a picture of this man in the reader's mind. And like a well prepared meal, these details should be seasoned within the dialogue, situations and actions that are taken throughout the story.

As if we are adding condiments to a meal, too much detail or salt for example and the meal is ruined, not enough and it lacks taste and can leave us feeling unsatisfied.

The dreaded info-dump is when we find out that Jason Harding was born on 18th May 1985, at Oxford John Radcliffe Hospital to parents Sarah and David at 4.30pm, by caesarian section and almost died, he fell asleep in the car on the way home, he was dropped on his head at 2 years old by his older brother, learnt to read by the age of 5, has a mark on his right hand where a dog bit him when he was six, he enjoyed macaroni cheese for his school lunch, his first girlfriend was Miranda at age 10 but she broke his heart by going off with his best friend... And the list goes on and on.

Readers often pick up a book for a moment of escapism from real life. A life where everything is dictated to them. By keeping your descriptions of places, people and scenarios detailed enough to understand but vague enough for your reader to draw their own conclusions about them, gives your reader the chance to participate in your story. There is a saying that three different people will tell the story of an incident three different ways and all of them will be right. Confused? No need to be. We all have our own perspective on what we see, do, hear and act on in life. Because of that, we all have our own bias's, our own agendas and our own point of view on things. All of them are right but we are all individuals. We see life through our own filters and nobody will ever truly see something the same as you do. Not even this post will be interpreted the same way by everyone. When you discover the freedom that brings as a writer, that's when the magic can happen.

Until next time, write on.

JR

Stick Or Twist? Does Your Novel Need Any More Drama?

How much is too much drama? How many times can you lead your reader to believe one thing before twisting it at the last minute? And if it's done too often, how far are you stretching reality?

When you start a new short story or novel, the blank page is a scary and exhilarating prospect. In a few short words you are about to send your protagonist out on an adventure that he/she/they may never survive or return from. It also begs the question, can you take things too far?

Granted, a reader is generally looking for some kind of escapism from the real world when they pick up your book but how far from the real world can you go whilst still making your storyline plausible to your audience? That can lie in the rhythm of your story and how well rounded you can make your characters appear as if they were real life people.

Whichever way we envisage our storylines in whatever genre we decide to write in, at the heart of it all is the imagined experience of a real character whether that be a human being, an animal, an alien etc. Even the most diabolical hated villain was once a normal average human being working to pay his way in life. They would have had family and friends around them. They would have had interests and hobbies that they enjoyed until something happened to them that flicked the switch in their mind and turned them into the villain they turned out to be in your story.

So how does this link into the drama side of the story? Whenever drama happens, there always needs to be a reason for it. Why is the building burning down? Why is there a car chase? In this example, why did this man/woman suddenly turn to a life of crime? And how far are you willing to go in order to justify the drama in your story?

A storyline needs to have its mix of ups and downs. It can't all be action, action, action all the way through, otherwise the 4th, 5th, 6th pieces of action will not have the same impact as the 1st, 2nd and 3rd did. Likewise, your story should not be all doom and gloom, mundane, basic, man/woman gets up, goes to work, eats a ham sandwich for lunch, goes home to their flat, feeds the cat, eats leftover curry from the night before and goes to bed. You'll end up boring your reader and they are likely to not finish your novel. Striking the right balance of ups and downs within your storyline is key to success.

The same can be said for plot twists and last line revelations. It can be a magnificent tool that you can use to lead your readers into believing one thing and then twisting it at the last minute to surprise them at the end. We do need to use this sparingly however. Although your readers are looking for escapism and if you have captured their attention with intriguing, authentic characters in marvellous locations on some kind of incredible adventure, there is only so far that you can push reality. The story still needs to have some kind of plausibility in it to satisfy your reader in the end.

Granted, in fantasy and science fiction novels, you have more creative licence to be more outrageous and extraordinary in your approach but your twist should not completely jolt your reader out of the storyline. After spending many hours and hundreds of pages with these characters, you need to craft a plausible, satisfying and in some cases, clever ending to your story. If you can manage that and leave your readers satisfied with your conclusions, they are more likely to pick up another one of your books and enjoy another adventure with you soon.

Until next time, write on.

JR

How Can I Make My Novel Flow?

My son recently had a writing project for his school homework and he asked me how he could make his story flow without it being too focused on action or becoming boring. This had me thinking about something that I learnt along the way of creating my Cornelius Cone adventures with my friend and co-author, Steve Boyce, and the Bennie Barrier adventures. The flow of these short stories is not one straight line from start to finish but a wavy flowing line of ups and downs.

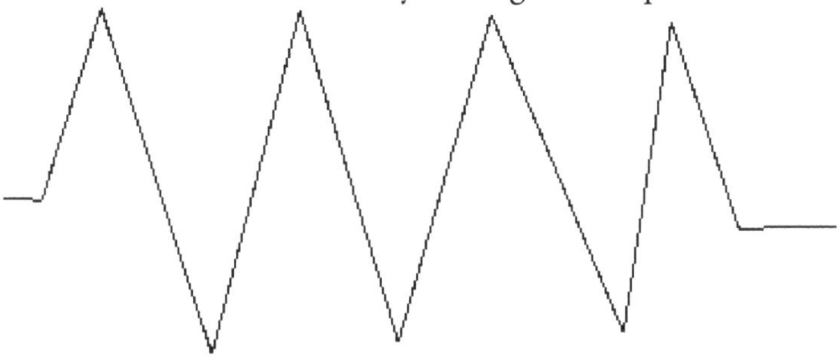

In order for a story to flow, it can't have too much of one thing without a counterbalance. In the example above, I asked my son to think of his main character, in this case, Captain Sandwich. We then drew the line where there were four up loops and three down loops. For the story to flow and have a rhythm, Captain Sandwich needed to have four good things happen to him that helped him on his quest and three bad things that caused conflict or stopped him from getting to where he needed to be.

To do this we started the novel introducing Captain Sandwich as part of a loaf of bread. He had been bought from the supermarket by Martha who had taken the bread home and had made cheese and tomato sandwiches for herself and her son, Frederick. The first "up" is Captain Sandwich being very happy that he was able to be used to create this cheese and tomato sandwich and has been placed in a lunchbox ready to be eaten on the family picnic. Now the first "down" point. When Frederick arrives at the park, he runs off to play with his friends, in turn, dropping his lunchbox which splits open. Martha picks up the contents of his lunchbox from the floor but doesn't realise that one of the sandwiches, in this case, Captain Sandwich is missing. Captain Sandwich is now on the grass in the park alone.

So, now we need another "up" part of the story. Captain Sandwich sees Martha and Frederick at the park. He notices the lunchbox on the park bench and runs over towards the bench thinking he is saved and how marvellous it is going to be to be part of the lunch again. Now, the next "down" point comes in. As he almost arrives at the park bench, a seagull swoops down and picks him up in her beak. Captain Sandwich is now upset because again he is no longer part of Frederick's lunch.

The seagull flies high above the park before landing on the branch of a tree. As the seagull lets Captain Sandwich go, his next "up" is his escape from the clutches of the seagull. He runs up the branch towards the tree trunk and jumps inside a hole where he follows a long tunnel down towards the base of the tree thinking that he has found an ingenious escape route.

From this, he discovers two squirrels inside the tree who think that Captain Sandwich has come along to steal their acorns. They then chase each other around the inside of the tree until Captain Sandwich escapes out into the park once again. Finally, after all of this, Captain Sandwich makes it back to the park bench where Frederick notices that he is on the floor. He picks Captain Sandwich up and hands him to Martha who notices that Captain Sandwich has been through quite an adventure and has become dirty from his exploits. He is then broken into pieces and fed to the dog as part of its lunch. As Captain Sandwich makes his way through the dog's body, he is satisfied that even though he wasn't part of Frederick's lunch he still completed his mission of being part of a lunchtime and will return to nature when the dog decides it's time for him to leave.

Now this flow of storyline, however basic it may seem to begin with, can be used as a template for your short stories and novels. A series of obstacles were put in Captain Sandwich's way to stop him from completing his objective from being part of the family's lunch. In the end, rather than being in Frederick's lunch, he ended up with the dog and that gave the story its twist at the end. Creating flow and the ups and downs of life gives a story its realism and authenticity. Life will never run smooth or exactly the way that you plan it and neither should your story. Prepare for the unexpected and embrace it, you never know what could happen next and that's the exciting bit.

Until next time, write on.

JR

How Important Is Character Development In A Novel?

What is most important to you when you write your novel or short story? Is it the plot? Location? Genre? The word count? Perhaps you've come up with this amazing, extraordinary idea that nobody has thought of but you need a vital ingredient if you are going to make your work a success. The missing ingredient is your characters. Whether they are people, animals, plants, aliens, whichever way your storyline goes, your characters and how they tell your story are key to its success or failure.

Most readers will pick up a book and look for a degree of escapism in the pages they read. This can be achieved in anything from a children's fairytale story through to the most graphic horror novel. We are looking to be entertained. Just having characters there for the sake of having characters isn't enough. They can come in all different forms; however, they must show some kind of character development as well as their actions dictating where the storyline is heading. Every decision needs to have a consequence as the dominoes begin to fall and the story reaches its conclusion.

I write a children's adventure series called Bennie Barrier's Big City Adventures. This follows on from the series that I co-wrote with my friend, Steve Boyce, featuring a local traffic cone called Cornelius Cone. The stories are based on what a traffic cone observes in his daily working life as well as his interactions with people and objects in his little village. With the Bennie series, I took a roadside barrier called Bennie and took him into the big city to see if he could prove himself away from the support of Cornelius Cone and all of his friends in Hythe Village. This is where Bennie's character development began. Just like when children move from Primary School to Secondary School, they suddenly go from being a big fish in a small pond to a small fish in a big pond. That was the adventure that Bennie Barrier encountered when he went to the big city. He met some nice new friends but he also met some others who were deceitful, nasty and untrustworthy too. The original plan of joining the City Maintenance Team didn't work out to start with and he ended up working in the loading bays of the city's shopping centre for a while. In putting Bennie in these different and often tricky circumstances, it enabled me to develop his character in ways that would not have been possible if he had stayed in the village with Cornelius Cone.

When developing an idea for a novel or short story, it is important to establish a beginning, a middle and an end. Your main character needs to have a starting point (Point A) and a satisfactory conclusion point (Point B). How they get from A to B is up to you. The messy middle can often go in all kinds of different directions but it is important that whichever way your creativity takes you, you always ensure that your point B, (the end point) is always the primary objective of the story. Failure to have a solid end point can often lead your storyline to go off on a tangent and you will end up with a half completed ramble that has very little or no direction.

Character development is key to achieving this. Your main character and his/her/their secondary characters should have their own story arc that changes them from how they were at the beginning of the story compared to how they are at the end. Going back to the escapism point from earlier, if you write about Mr or Mrs Average who drive a beige car to the supermarket everyday, buy the same groceries, speak to the same people, go home and eat the same lunch, follow the same daily rituals and then go to bed just to repeat the same routine over and over again, you're going to bore your reader. They will lose interest and give up on your work. With so many different forms of media competing for the attention of those who may take a chance on your book, you need your writing to be as absorbing, extraordinary and escapist as it can be. You need to drag your readers out of their everyday life and into the lives of your amazing characters, leaving your readers wishing that they could actually meet them and be their friends in real life. If you can develop your characters in such a way that you make them real in the minds of those who encounter them, that is something special.

Don't be afraid to make your characters seem extraordinary. A lot of novels are based in a world that seems normal to those who read and experience the world that you have built for your characters. The more authentic and realistic you can create these worlds in the minds of your readers, the more likely they are to believe that your character can do extraordinary things. Have you ever encountered a situation where, in hindsight, you wish you had said or done something differently that would have changed the outcome? Your characters have the chance to do that. To have the courage to speak up. To have the confidence to do something outrageous. The power is in your hands. Develop your characters and your literary world is your oyster. Have fun with it.

Until next time, write on.

JR

How Do You Know What Genre To Write In?

Genres can easily become box-ticking exercises that debut authors can become pigeon-holed into because they feel they need to fit into one. The truth is, unless you are already writing for an ongoing series such as Sherlock Holmes or James Bond for example, the story you are about to write will be unique to you.

Publishing houses will often look for commercialisation of your manuscript and unfortunately, in some circumstances, this will mean a considerable rewrite of your story that bears little resemblance to what you had originally planned. Self publishing or partnership publishing will give you a lot more freedom regarding the type of story you want to write and will be less focused on the current trends of what is popular at the time of your novel/short story hitting the market.

Most authors will want to have their book in shops in the hope of generating vast sales that will lead them into the position of making writing their full time career and a lucky few do have that result. To do this, marketing is a key element whenever you are looking to sell your book and therefore, the customer will need to have an understanding of what your book entails. For example, a horror novel would be unsuitable in the childrens books section but getting too hung up on being genre specific can often dilute the creativity of an author when writing their manuscript.

Personally, I have co-written The New Adventures Of Cornelius Cone And Friends with my friend Steve Boyce as well as the new Bennie Barrier's Big City Adventures series which came out at the beginning of 2024. Both of these series are a collection of short stories aimed at Primary School children about the Maintenance Workers that they would have often seen on the roads in their local area. The village and city where the cones and barriers live are loosely based in the city of Southampton and the village of Hythe near The New Forest on England's south coast. The adventures these character embark on and the places they visit show the scenarios through a child's viewpoint and can vary from mild crime, mystery, ghost stories, humour and in some cases, complete fantasy where Cornelius Cone and Bennie Barrier are transported to a magical world after they are sucked into a mural that had been painted on the wall of a local building. Although these stories are under the umbrella of the "Children's Stories" genre, they are a combination of different storylines and genres encapsulated into two complete series.

The contrast that I find with my writing has allowed me to explore many different genres in my adult fiction as well. Recently, I have been asked by a friend to consider writing a fantasy novel which I have plans to start in 2025 and I have a crime thriller series called "The Blake Langford Adventures" which I am currently editing the fourth novel of as well.

The more varied the genres are, the more I seem to be able to learn about my writing style, world building and characterisation as I take on these new projects. If you stick too rigidly to a genre, your writing runs the risk of being a "paint-by-numbers" procedural that could easily become formulaic and a cliche of what has gone before. Your writing, your ideas and your unique perspective deserves more than that. Create an outline of the story you want to write, build your structure around that, research well, make your characters as authentic as you can to the storyline and circumstances that you place them in and run with it. Have fun and see where your story takes you without having to constantly follow the troupes that have gone before. Your story is unique. Its genre will work itself out later. The important thing is that you write it and share it with the world. You never know who may be reading it...

Until next time, write on.

JR

I Haven't Wrote Anything For A Month, Have I Lost My Motivation?

We all get it don't we? You sit down at the laptop or with your notebook and stare at the blank page. You've set aside a couple of hours to write and.... Nothing. The muse just won't come. Ideas dry up. You wonder; what's the point? You stare at the page a little longer before pushing it away in frustration and lose yourself into a slew of social media, perhaps venting that you're a failure and can't do what you want to do. Have you lost your motivation or is it something else?

We are all familiar with the term, "Writer's Block." For a lot of people, it becomes this nemesis that plagues them throughout their writing career where, for whatever reason, the words just won't flow. You can't seem to figure out where your story is heading. To combat this, I have what I call my scribble book. It's a cheap notepad that you can buy from most shops and in that book, I write out everything which is on my mind. Others often refer to this as their diary where they journal their daily lives, their hopes and dreams and their objectives for now and the future but in this scribble book, I simply look to declutter my mind. Even if none of it makes sense. Just write about anything and everything. You'll be amazed how much emotional traffic we carry in our minds subconsciously without even realising it.

From this notebook of seemingly random thoughts often comes a key trigger that can be used at a later date. Our subconscious is often trying to tell us things but we are too wrapped up in our everyday lives to listen to what our mind is trying to say. Never throw away anything that could potentially give you a great idea for a future project further down the line.

In general, I try to write something everyday in order to keep my mind focused on the project that I am working on. Even if I only create a sentence or paragraph. Progress is still progress no matter how small and it is much easier to edit a full page than an empty one. Occasionally however, and this is usually when we decide to go on holiday abroad, I will have a two or three week spell where I am not writing at all. In the past, I would have been worried about losing my flow, not being able to continue on from where I left off, but the fear of this is often what leads to us being unproductive and encouraging the inevitable writer's block. By actually embracing the fact that I will not be producing any kind of writing for up to three weeks actually allows my mind to switch off and focus on other things in my life. How often do we walk down the street and not notice the wind in the trees, people passing by, beautiful countryside or beaches as we zoom past in our cars rushing to get from A to B?

As with anything in life, too much of something can often be unhealthy. If we overwork, overeat, over-indulge in anything, it can often become routine and boring. Your favourite artist has just released an amazing new song that you've had on repeat for the past couple of weeks. This song that you absolutely loved will soon become just another member of the playlist/CD or collection of music that you have created over the years. Sometimes, you just need a break in order to appreciate something again and when you hear that same song a year from now, you will love it all over again and the same goes for writing.

If you are struggling to find your writing muse at the moment, try something different. Blogging, fan-fiction, character profiles, reading a book outside of the normal genres you would read. Inspiration can spring up from anywhere at any time. Step out of the ordinary and let extraordinary things happen. Don't lose the faith, you have the ability to be an amazing writer, give yourself a break and then go for it, you can do it!

Until next time, write on.

JR

If You've Never Been To A Writing Festival Before, Do It!

At the end of April 2024, I attended the Bournemouth Writing Festival. Being a first time visitor of one of these festivals, I wasn't sure of what to expect. What I discovered surpassed all of my expectations.

From the friendly welcome to engaging with other writers at different stages of their writing journey. There were publishers willing to discuss traditional, partnership and self publishing options with equal importance and the inspiration generated by being within a group of like minded individuals was incredible.

Whatever writing project you put your mind to, it can be an often daunting and lonely experience staring at a screen for hours in the hope that you are able to create a masterpiece worthy of the appraisal of your readers. There can also be many pitfalls along the way such as vanity publishing companies as well as, if you go down the traditional publishing route, surrendering all of the rights to your work. A subject rarely discussed but at the festival, nothing was off of the table.

Various publishers can offer different levels of service. The most popular tends to be Amazon KDP which offers writers a free self publishing route into the market. This may sound inviting however, you are then responsible for your own editing, marketing, distribution to bookshops and every aspect of your publishing journey. Now, compared to some of the distribution companies out there, Amazon has by far the largest reach. In terms of users and books sold by the company, Amazon is the hypermarket whilst other web based distribution services are more of a market stall. The ease in which Amazon allows books to be published though means that there is a huge saturation in the self publishing market. Over a million books are self published by them every year. That means that when you release your book into this market, you have to promote it as if your book's success depended on it because believe me, it will. A huge social media following, relentless promotion and paid ads will get you so far but you have to put yourself out there to make it happen.

The alternatives, as discussed at the festival were partnership publishing models where a publisher will share half of the costs of producing, distributing and publishing your book and the traditional publishing route where an advance is paid to the author for their book and all of the costs accompanying the publishing journey are absorbed by the publisher. Sounds good but there are some caveats to consider with the traditional route. Unless you are a well established author or a celebrity, the odds of traditional publishing houses taking a chance on your book are very slim. Publishing is a business and like any business, the traditional publishers need to make money to survive. No book can be a guaranteed success, however, the traditional publishing houses will make an educated guess on whether the book will sell enough to cover the advance they give to the author and their own costs. Therefore, it often comes down to a popularity contest. A celebrity or well established author can command sales in the thousands where a new author delivering their first book to the market often will struggle to hit the hundreds. Unfortunately it is a numbers game that the author is unlikely to win.

As well as this, traditional publishers will tend to buy the entire rights to your book. This therefore means that you will have little or no say in the book cover and they will be able to change significant sections of your novel to make your story commercially successful for the market at the time of publication. Partnership publishing however gives you more control over the content of your book as well as its cover, distribution and marketing. This however can come at a cost so it is up to you how much you are really willing to invest in your book to make your dream of being a published author a reality.

So, overall, The Bournemouth Writing Festival was a fantastic experience. From getting out there and meeting likeminded people who are working on their own projects to established authors and those who simply have a passing interest and are looking for inspiration, it is an informative and inclusive event that I will be attending for many years to come. Especially since the pandemic, online writing groups have been springing up all over the place and having a sense of community around you can give writers some amazing encouragement. A lot of these groups are happening on social media and it can be an invaluable source for new writers looking for illustrators, editors and marketing experts. Of course, nobody can guarantee that your writing will be a commercial success and every venture you undertake is somewhat of a gamble but for the lucky few, it can be a great source of additional income and a gateway into a career that they had often dreamed of.

If you have ever dreamt of being a writer, of creating magical lands for your readers to escape to and of sharing your ideas with the world, these festivals can be a marvellous way to let your inspiration take you on that journey. So, what are you waiting for, make a difference, put pen to paper and write! You won't regret it.

Until next time, write on.

JR

How Can You Place Yourself In Someone Else's Situation And Make Them The Focus Of Your Story?

We all have a story inside us. Cliche? Trite? Stay with me on this. No matter who you are, what stage you are at in life, you lead a life that is unique to you. From the time you wake up until the time you go to bed, the things you do, the places you go, the people you see, the conversations you have, the actions you take, they are all unique to you. There is not another person in this world that is identical to you and because of that, you are unique and from the day you were born until now, things have happened to you. Whether they are good, bad, indifferent, it doesn't matter. These thoughts and memories could make you happy or sad, the point is, you experienced them from your own unique viewpoint and they all come together to make the story of you.

So how do you put yourself into the place of somebody else and make them the focus of your story? In fact, as a male, forty year old author myself, I am currently working on a project for 2025/26 where the main character in my new crime thriller series is a thirty year old woman who has had to fight her way through a male dominated world to be the best at what she does. Naturally, being a male my whole life, I have little knowledge or experience of how women were treated throughout the nineties and up to the present day and this is where, talking to people in the profession you are writing about and talking to women in those kinds of environments can be valuable research into how a woman can make the difference in a seemingly "man's world."

When I travel on public transport, I see many people getting on and off of trains and buses and often try to figure out a story in my mind of what their lives could be like. A lot of our imagination and influences will come from the books we read, the films we watch and the media we consume and a lot of the time, our imagination tends to run away with itself. For example, the man in the sharp suit may not have necessarily been an agent in a James Bond film or the elderly man with a walking stick and a long white beard is not necessarily a wizard or on his way back from Mount Doom in Lord Of The Rings. However, we never truly see behind the mask that people show the world so, the flustered mother with two young children struggling to take her shopping home on a Friday evening could be an inspiration for a story. Is she a carer? Does she have a partner at home? Is she a single mother? Is she scared and in a violent relationship? What set of circumstances has led to her being there at that particular moment on that day?

By using a combination of research into the subject matter you are pursuing and your own personal experiences, it is possible to place yourself into the life of your fictional character in a way that will be authentic and memorable. By using people you encounter in day-to-day life as a potential template for the basis of your character, you can build up a picture in your mind and most importantly in the minds of your readers where they can identify with your characters as if they are real people.

By creatively building up your character's profile so the reader can imagine how they will look, how they will react to other people and scenarios and any number of given circumstances in the world you create within your story, you can effectively place yourself into somebody else's world. The escapism that readers crave when they pick up a book is to escape their real world for a while and delve into the lives of their favourite characters in an alternative world. By giving them the doorway into this magical place, as an author, you will capture their attention and hopefully, their future readership for many more adventures to come. Use it wisely.

Until next time, write on.

JR

I Want To Write A Book But I Don't Know Where To Start

This is one that I get a lot. A friend of mine wanted to write his life story however he didn't know where to start. With this being my first non-fiction work, it was difficult to plan out how I would approach blogging about writing. After much thought and procrastination, I finally decided to just write what came naturally whether it made sense or not.

This can be a great cure for writer's block too. I have a scribble book where I just write out random thoughts and ideas, most of which will never see the light of day, however, it does seem to declutter my mind from what's been happening in the world around me.

As writers we are great at procrastination. We come to a stumbling block within the story and go to Google to research, for example, the UK living wage in 1948 and come back an hour later after several social media scrolls, several emails answered, feeding the dog, making a cup of coffee and checking the football results. A lot of the time, the most effective way to begin is to plant your butt on the seat, open your notebook or laptop and write.

I currently have two children's adventure series, one adult crime fiction series and two potential new projects planned in for the future that I am looking forward to starting very soon but a lot of the time, I try to absorb information and advice from my peers along the way. Courses on writing such as the new BBC Maestro and Open University Creative Writing courses can be a great source of not only teaching potential authors how to improve their writing and increase their chances of publication but also, to fire up the imagination inside you.

Having several projects on the go at the same time can have its benefits and its downfalls. If I find myself struggling on one, I tend to switch over to another before returning later to the original task, quite often with a different viewpoint and the story moves off into a direction that I never expected. When I started out, I was very much one project and one story at a time.

I wrote a few magazine articles in 2008 but until 2020, I had barely given writing a second thought until my friend, Steve Boyce, created his fantastic illustrated Cornelius Cone adventures that captured the imagination of my son. From these stories, we came up with some ideas of other adventures that Cornelius and his friends could embark on and, with Steve's permission, I set about writing these adventures, firstly for my son and later to become part of the Cornelius Cone series that we share together.

So if you are eager to begin your writing career but do not want to commit to a writing course, from my own experience, a good place to start is by looking for inspiration in things you enjoy reading and watching on TV. Obviously many programs have their own copyright which should never be abused or plagiarised, however, as a kickstarter to begin your creative writing journey, there are many ways in which these influences can help you. For example, if you are a huge Only Fools And Horses fan, how about writing your own episode? A fan-fiction version where you decide what Del, Rodney and Uncle Albert get up to next. Or maybe you're more of a soap fan. Could you potentially write a new episode of Eastenders or Coronation Street? In using these templates as a means of practising your writing style, you have a clear idea in your mind of who these characters are, how they look, how they react in any given circumstances and the world they populate. From this, you can use the same kind of ideas to launch your own series whether that be in novel or script writing. Your unique idea could potentially lead to a series that has not been thought of or created yet.

The best advice to start off with that I could give is to write what you enjoy and use the stories you read, the films you watch and the media you consume to create your own world where your unique characters can thrive. Make notes along the way to keep your storyline consistent and let your creative mind flow. You'll be surprised how far you can go if you have the courage to start.

Until next time, write on.

JR

When Creating Your Villain, Why Should Their Back Story Align With Their Motives?

We all enjoy a good villain in our favourite film, TV series or novel but how can you create a memorable villain who is grounded in reality? The answer is more in their psychology than just someone who is inherently evil.

When creating your villain, you need to understand what made that person decide to do what they do? What set of circumstances would drive a normal, well-rounded individual to commit these crimes? To do this, you often need to firstly look at yourself. Even the most placid, law-abiding citizens among us have our limits. So what would it take for you to turn evil? What would have to happen to you that pushes you too far?

The beauty of being an author is that even though our influences and life experiences shape the person we are today, we have an opportunity to create a fascinating, complex and absorbingly authentic magical world for our characters. Likewise, we create a cast of characters who embody that world. Your villainous character, no matter what age, height, build, ethnicity or privilege was once an innocent law-abiding child/teen/adult. Then something changed. An injustice. Something was done to this individual that led them onto a destructive path which has led them to this place in your story.

This can be explored in so many ways. Do they have a deep down childhood trauma? Were they abused or did their parents tragically die whilst he/she was young? Did they have an abusive parent? Was alcohol, drugs or violence at play in their childhood? Were they the overweight unpopular nerdy child at school who was mercilessly bullied by the bigger kids until one day, they finally snapped and took retribution?

Maybe they have just had their first sexual relationship and then they discover that their partner has cheated on them? Perhaps they have been married for years, have their own children and then suddenly discover that their partner has a secret life they didn't know about.

Another angle could be a terminal illness or something that happened to them that has changed their way of life and their dreams of the future. Were they in a car accident? Have they lost a limb due to someone else's negligence? Have they received a terminal cancer diagnosis yet they see young men and women wasting their lives away on drugs and alcohol? Have they been married for many years and then suddenly, their partner died or was murdered?

Any of these events and many that I haven't mentioned could be enough to tip the average person into a life of crime. We come across so many people in our daily lives. When you visit the supermarket to do your weekly grocery shopping, there is a good chance that you will encounter twenty or thirty people in that supermarket living their own lives, with their own responsibilities and problems. Any one of them could potentially suffer a life changing event that pushes them to their limit or even beyond it.

Keeping your villain grounded in reality is key to the authenticity of your story. Obviously, if you are writing cartoonish characters such as Batman or any of the well established tropes, there are exceptions but for your readers to connect and really relate to your villain, you need to have a deep understanding of their motives and what drove them from placid to crazy.

So, when you look to create your memorable villain, keep in mind, what would drive YOU to commit the crimes they are about to do? Is there a serial killer inside of you given the right circumstances? I guess we'll never know.

Until next time, write on.

JR

I've Always Wanted To Write A Novel But I Never Have The Time... How Do You Create Your Masterpiece In Today's Hectic World?

When I decide to tell people that I am an author, I often get asked, "how do you find the time to do it?" Well, the answer is more straightforward than you might think. Let's break things down a little here; how long on average do you spend each day scrolling social media and videos on your phone? How long do you spend watching TV in the evenings? If you use public transport for your commute to work, what are you doing with the time when you are on the bus or train?

Add these elements of your average day up and you'll be surprised how much time you waste doing things that have little or no value to you. I tend to see my writing as a hobby that occasionally will make me some extra cash on the side. Even in our information loaded, hectic lives we lead in 2024; people will always find the time to do something they want to do. If you regularly listen to a podcast, go to the gym, meet your friend for coffee mornings; these are part of your routine. To cut out a section of time from your schedule to write, you need to firstly WANT to write and secondly, include writing time into your daily routine.

Generally, it is said to take 28 days to create a habit. In writing terms, a good way to kick start this is with the November writing collaboration known as NaNoWriMo, which stands for National Novel Writing Month. You don't necessarily need to wait until November to implement the practices for this collaboration however, if you are looking for online support and encouragement then this November, why not take up the challenge.

So, what is NaNoWriMo? Every November, writers around the world commit to writing up to fifty-thousand words in the 30 days of the month. That means that as a writer, you will need to commit time every single day of November to write a minimum of 1667 words per day. This is not a set number. Some days can be more, some less, some days it may be impossible to write any, but the target is still there; fifty-thousand words by the time the clock strikes midnight on November 30th.

This can be especially good if you are a writer who is a perfectionist or tends to procrastinate a lot. The knowledge of having to hit a word count each day means you don't have time to hang around. The aim is to get as close to that fifty-thousand word target as possible so that you have a body of work to edit and hopefully use as a first draft of a potential novel.

In 2023, I attempted, and failed, NaNoWriMo as family commitments derailed my plans of writing the fifty-thousand words in 30 days however, the amount of writing that I did achieve created a significant part of the first draft of my latest Blake Langford novel; Wheel Of Deception. For anyone who has an idea for a novel, my advice would be to write out a rough plan of your storyline and then use the NaNoWriMo model and go for it. Write as much as you can and then edit at will. Like many people say, you can edit a bad page, you can't edit a blank page.

So, finding the time to write is basically down to what is important to you each day. We often prioritise things that we enjoy so why can't writing be part of that too? When you're scrolling social media this evening, why not set an alarm on your phone, pick up a notepad and a pen and start writing. You'll be amazed how quickly ideas can develop and how you can find your flow. Remember, the first draft is never perfect and only you are going to read that first effort. Get your ideas down on paper or on your screen, let the words flow and see where the muse takes you. You may even surprise yourself.

Until next time, write on.

JR

Conclusion

So, if you've reached this far, I congratulate and thank you for your support. This was never my intention to publish my weekly rambles, however, I hope they managed to inspire, confuse, invigorate and irritate everyone who made the decision to read them.

This collection is my first year of blogging on Substack and I will be continuing my weekly blog of writing tidbits and pieces of wisdom going into 2025.

If you would like to continue with the journey, please feel free to give me a follow on JohnRobertsAuthor.Substack.com

I wish you the very best of luck in your writing journey and hopefully I'll see you at a writing event very soon.

Until next time, write on.

JR

The Blake Langford Adventures

John Roberts is the author of the crime thriller series; The Blake Langford Adventures.

Catch up with the series so far from most online retailers.

Where No One Stands Alone

Underneath The Covers

In The Shadow Of My Life

Wheel Of Deception

Everything

Questions For The Dead

Home For September

Pieces Of My Life

Children's Books By John Roberts & Steve Boyce

John Roberts is also the author of the new Bennie Barrier's Big City Adventures series and a co-author of the Amazon children's book series; The New Adventures Of Cornelius Cone And Friends with his friend, Steve Boyce. Over 80 ebooks are currently available as well as 18 paperback and hardback compilations.

Bennie Barrier's Big City Adventures - Volume 1

Bennie Barrier's Big City Adventures - Volume 2

The New Adventures Of Cornelius Cone And Friends - Part One

The New Adventures Of Cornelius Cone And Friends - Part Two

The New Adventures Of Cornelius Cone And Friends - Part Three

The New Adventures Of Cornelius Cone And Friends - Part Four

The New Adventures Of Cornelius Cone And Friends - Part Five

The New Adventures Of Cornelius Cone And Friends - Part Six

The New Adventures Of Cornelius Cone And Friends - Part Seven

The New Adventures Of Cornelius Cone And Friends - Part Eight

The New Adventures Of Cornelius Cone And Friends - Part Nine

The New Adventures Of Cornelius Cone And Friends - Part Ten

The Whole Cone

The Whole Cone 2 - Above The High Visibility Belt

Cornelius Cone And Friends - The Story So Far - Volume One

Cornelius Cone And Friends - The Story So Far - Volume Two

Cornelius Cone And Friends - The Story So Far - Volume Three

Cornelius Cone And Friends - The Story So Far - Volume Four

The New Adventures Of Cornelius Cone And Friends Novel - The Return Of Susie Suitcase

Bennie Barrier's Best Bits: My Adventures With A Cone Named Cornelius

Susie Suitcase's Selected Stories: My Encounters With A Cone Named Cornelius

Postman Pete's Predicaments: A Catalogue Of Errors With A Cone Named Cornelius

Tricia Trolley's Tea Time Treats: Bitesize Tales With A Cone Named Cornelius

For all the latest John Roberts news, please visit the website: www. CorneliusCone.co.uk